Pastor as Counselor

D1557135

Other Books by John Patton

Pastoral Care: An Essential Guide

Christian Marriage and Family: Caring for Our Generations

Is Human Forgiveness Possible? A Pastoral Care Perspective

Pastoral Care in Context: An Introduction to Pastoral Care

Dictionary of Pastoral Care and Counseling (Associate Editor)

From Ministry to Theology: Pastoral Action and Reflection

Pastoral Counseling: A Ministry of the Church

Pastor as Counselor

Wise Presence, Sacred Conversation

John Patton

Abingdon Press™

Nashville

Library of Congress Cataloging-in-Publication Data

Patton, John, 1930-
　　Pastor as counselor : wise presence, sacred conversation / John Patton.—First [edition].
　　　pages cm
　　Includes bibliographical references.
　　ISBN 978-1-63088-690-5 (binding: pbk.j)
　　1. Pastoral counseling.　I. Title.
　　BV4012.2.P349 2015
　　253.5—dc23

2015014497

Scripture quotations are from the Common English Bible. Copyright © 2011 by the Common English Bible. All rights reserved. Used by permission. www.CommonEnglishBible.com.

15 16 17 18 19 20 21 22 23 24—10 9 8 7 6 5 4 3 2 1
MANUFACTURED IN THE UNITED STATES OF AMERICA

Contents

Contents

Introduction

This book is intended to be a conversation with pastors about the kind of pastoral counseling that they can and should provide. The goal of the book is to aid the practice of those ministers whose setting for ministry is the congregation, the armed services, or institutions other than counseling centers. It deals with the kind of counseling that can best be thought of as consultation on life and meaning from a religious perspective. Pastoral counseling may in some ways be thought of as a spiritual practice, but the language it uses is not primarily religious. Rather, in most cases, it involves practical talk about life in ordinary, everyday language that has more of the character of the biblical book of Proverbs than the book of Psalms. Since pastors are female and male, rather than repeatedly using "he or she," I will be alternating their gender designation from chapter to chapter. In this introduction and in chapter 1 the pastor will be male. In chapter 2, she will be female and so on.

The premise of the book is that the minister who is not specially trained in mental health counseling can offer wise presence and spiritual conversation to persons who are in some way separated and lost from significant persons and places. The counseling that the pastor offers is based primarily on being there in relationship as a person who represents a God who cares. What the pastor does in counseling grows out of that image and experience. It is based on a faith in the power of such interpersonal care to make life better. As a part of his regular, noncounseling ministry a pastor has a great deal of experience with personal, group, and family relationships. If he can respect what he does know about interpersonal relationships and continue to develop it, he can be an effective counselor for individuals and families.

While leading a seminar for clergy leaders who were involved in supervising or consulting with other clergy, I presented the case of a person being supervised in his ministry who was confronted with a number of difficult to impossible situations to deal with. After several of the group members struggled to say what they would do to solve the problem, one of the older members of the group, a bishop, said with conviction, "I don't know what I would do, but I'd be there."

The conviction of the pastoral tradition is that the need for a caring relationship exists whatever the presenting problem may be. The type of counseling that I write about in this book is a "being there" kind of pastoral care that takes place within the structure of a counseling interview. It is care that becomes pastoral counseling when the initiative for it comes from the person or persons needing help rather than from the pastor and the community the pastor represents.

The wisdom about relationships early in the pastor's career grows primarily out of what he represents and later out of his experience with persons and groups in his overall ministry. This experience is described in this book as relational wisdom. Relational wisdom contributes to what is frequently called spiritual care in chaplaincy circles, but it clearly grows out of the images and faith of the Christian tradition. It is founded upon a shared faith in a relational God who is present in all our relationships with a shepherd's care for both the entire flock and the individual sheep who, for varying reasons, find themselves cut off from the supportive experience of the community. Although today most people are less familiar with a term from rural life like *pastoral*, the experience of "lostness" from relationship to what is most important to them is as relevant today as it once was.

The book grows out of experience in counseling with persons from a variety of religious backgrounds and is intended to reach beyond one faith tradition. The guidance it gives about what is most important in the practice of counseling, however, grows out of the Christian tradition's view of the meaning and importance of pastoral care. What the counseling pastors should be doing is not essentially different or separate from the pastoral care they offer to individual persons and families and in the oversight of their religious communities. It is simply one of the ways that the Christian pastoral tradition of care is expressed through counsel to persons who acknowledge in some way that they are out of touch with the resources they need for dealing with their lives.

The modern pastoral counseling movement developed in the years after World War II in response to problems related to what we now call post-traumatic stress disorder. At that time there was a need for more mental health counselors. In response to that need, training in explicit psychologically informed counseling began to be developed in seminaries and in various centers for the clinical education of theological students and clergy.

The situation in the world today is both similar and different. It is similar in that we are still dealing with many human problems related to the stress of war, and we continue to need counselors who are knowledgeable about this and the family issues related to it. The situation is different, however, in that there are now many more counselors available—counselors who have been trained to deal with mental health problems through particular skills and techniques.

Partly because there are more counselors today, there is a common assumption that all human problems should be handled by specialists who are trained to deal with specific mental health problems. Because of this narrowed focus on what effective counseling should be, many ministers, both parish pastors and institutional chaplains, assume that if they don't have training to deal with mental health problems they should not do any kind of counseling. For them, counseling has become something they do not understand as part of their vocation in ministry.

This is unfortunate in today's world where the ability of persons to be technically in touch with one another has radically increased but where contact through technology is constantly being substituted for direct, more personal relationships. There are many people who seem to stop at the fact of contact rather than moving beyond that toward more significant relationships. It is in this kind of technically efficient but often impersonal world that pastoral counseling can be a radical counterpoint and correction.

A major purpose of this book is to counteract that overspecialized understanding of counseling as something so specialized that ministers should not be involved in it. The book affirms the importance of a pastoral tradition that says the need for care exists in our response to all human problems and that pastors as counselors have an important ministry in a type of counseling that is simply an extension of what they do in their pastoral care. The world in which the pastoral tradition is carried out is populated with all kinds of specialists who have particular knowledge and skills applicable to the problems of the individual person. Because of what is, perhaps, an overconcern with specialization, it may be important for the pastors also to think of themselves as having a specialty. In what way, then, can the pastor be thought of as a specialist? To be sure, pastors are trained in biblical studies, theology, and spirituality and, to some degree, in ethics, but I believe that their real specialty is in the practice that can appropriately be called "relational wisdom"—wisdom about relationships with persons and with God that is part of the pastoral tradition that the minister represents.

For many years in my writing and teaching I have echoed something I first heard from Baptist pastoral theologian Wayne Oates: *pastoral counseling is a ministry of availability and introduction.* For many people, mental health treatment is out there somewhere, not much related to them, and making them anxious to consider. The religious community is generally nearer and more available, even for those who are not members of it. It is important, therefore, that pastors be available to respond to persons with all kinds of difficult human situations.

This response does not mean that pastors must be the ones to finish the counseling task as well as begin it. Rather, as a minister of introduction, the pastor needs to know when to *defer* to others and how to *refer* to various kinds of specialists in a way that is as personal as possible. And in doing this, pastors can maintain and affirm the ongoing relationship of their religious community's care about the psychological counseling that may take place outside it.

In many ways this "how to do it book" tells pastors what they need to think about and do in their pastoral counseling as the bearer of relational wisdom. What I say here I have said in pastoral care classes and seminars over the years. However, this kind of specific, sometimes nearly dogmatic, book about what to do is not sufficient for learning the practice of counseling. Reading must be paired with ongoing consultation with particular pastors about specific life situations in which they are trying to offer help and in relation to their own particular style of ministry. The pastoral reader is bringing some experience in care and counseling to the dialogue about the specific things they need to think about and do in pastoral counseling. One of the most important things I will be saying is that good pastoral counseling is something that requires a plan and a structure in order to be effective. I don't expect the reader to agree with all the things that I say about this, but I hope to be definite and clear enough to stir some dialogue about what should be prepared for and done in the counseling by the pastor who is not specifically trained in pastoral counseling.

The book's title affirms that pastoral counseling is about "wise presence" and "sacred conversation." I have already touched upon and will discuss in more detail later the importance of presence and the meaning of the relational wisdom that a pastor can offer. What the very practical discussion of how to do pastoral counseling has to do with "sacred conversation" is another question. I suggested earlier that pastoral counseling is a spiritual practice that most often uses language that is not primarily religious. Rather, in most cases, it involves practical talk about life in ordinary, everyday language and affirms that an important part of what guides the pastoral counselor is the ability to discern echoes of the sacred in language of everyday life.

The first chapter, "The Pastor's Specialty: Relational Wisdom," of this book discusses why persons come to ministers for counsel and what they may get from counseling that is pastoral. It affirms that what may be gained from pastoral counseling is associated with the positive kind of life and life's meaning that the religious community and the pastor represent. The chapter offers a reinterpretation of the kind of person a pastor is expected to be as it is presented in one of the later books of the New

Testament. In describing what a pastor can offer in pastoral counseling there is a discussion of the meanings of the terms *pastoral, counsel,* and *wisdom,* noting particularly how they contribute to developing wisdom that is relational.

The second chapter begins the "how to do it" section of the book. It describes how the pastor can effectively structure the first pastoral counseling meeting with a person seeking help. Again, it is very specific about the way things should be done but attempts to do this in a way that invites dialogue with the pastoral reader by asking him to think about what his way of beginning a session might be and to consider some alternatives. The chapter continues to express the view that pastoral counseling is, in fact, pastoral care—something the pastor already knows something about—but it is different because of its definite structure for the way the meeting is to be conducted and because the person needing help was the one who initiated it.

This first meeting with the counselee is concerned with arriving at an initial understanding of the person or persons present and the problem they present. It further involves the pastor and counselee or counselees in making a decision together about how to explore the concerns that have been revealed in the limited time they will have together for this purpose. Part of the pastor's task is to convey at the beginning of counseling meetings that his time for counseling is limited to no more than three or four sessions and that referral to a more specialized counselor will be a definite part of what they are considering together.

The third chapter is concerned with what happens if the counselee and the pastor have decided that they should meet again for counseling. It begins with a follow-up of some of the things that happened in the first meeting or in between that meeting and this one. It continues through what is called both "care-full" and "bifocal" listening: "care-full" in its understanding of this meeting to be a part of pastoral care and "bi-focal" in that it is concerned not only about the problem but also about the larger life situation of the counselee. Also involved is some attention to ways of determining the degree of anxiety and depression that the person is experiencing. The kinds of things that the pastor does in this kind of evaluation are designed to decide, along with the counselee, how much further he should go on in counseling this person or whether the focus should be on an effective referral to a specialist in mental health.

The fourth chapter focuses more specifically upon the counselee's relationships, ways of thinking about them and dealing with them. The pastor's concern with families is with all their generations, past, present, and future, and with the way the generations attempt to care for each other. Parish ministers, particularly, are constantly dealing with families at all stages of life. It is important that they value that experience, develop it further, and use it in counseling through the structure of family conferences with couples or with members of all generations of the family. If pastors can respect their experience without thinking of themselves as family therapists or savers of marriages, they can offer an effective ministry through their counseling.

The fifth chapter addresses a number of family-related problems that the pastor may be consulted about: balancing work and family responsibilities, family-like problems at work, becoming a peer in one's own generation, achieving an adult-adult relationship with parents, physical and emotional abuse through addiction and infidelity, family decisions about matters of life and death. As the last chapter of the book, this chapter will conclude with a summary of the book's argument about why and how parish ministers and others whose ministry is not primarily in counseling should do counseling as pastors. It concludes with both a reminder about how important it is for the pastor to have a trusted consultant or consultation group they are a part of and a list of further readings that may contribute to further developing the pastor's relational wisdom.

The book assumes that ministers, whatever the primary emphasis of their ministry, will at times be sought out for counsel and will want to respond to that request in a helpful way.

Chapter One

The Pastor's Specialty:
Relational Wisdom

The pastor's counseling offers a "wise presence" and "spiritual conversation" to persons who are in some way lost or separated from what is meaningful in their lives. Although the chapters of the book that follow this one are specific in prescribing what the pastor should do in his counseling, what is said there is not dependent on learning a particular mental health type of counseling but upon being there in relationship as a person who represents a God who cares for the one who has asked for help. What the pastor does is based on faith in the power of such care to make life better.

I believe that the pastor's education and experience in ministry provide an unusual opportunity to develop wisdom about personal, group, and family relationships. If he can avoid being intimidated by what he does not know about counseling and psychotherapy, make use of what he represents, claim what he has already learned in his ministry about relationships, and be committed to further development, he can be an effective counselor for individuals and families.

The world today is populated with all kinds of specialists. Pastors practice what can be called "relational wisdom"—a wisdom about relationships with persons and with God that is part of the pastoral tradition that the minister represents. Ministers who offer pastoral counsel may not initially possess a great deal of wisdom understood in this relational way,

Know your boundaries.

but because of what they represent to persons seeking help, the wisdom they have developed may be enough to allow them to be effective in their counseling.

The pastor's specialty in "relational wisdom" grows out of the Christian pastoral tradition's belief in a God who cares for persons and who empowers the caring behavior of members of its faith communities for ministry to persons both inside and outside of it. Certainly, that caring is not the only purpose of religious communities, but it continues to be one of the most important, particularly today. It is important not only for counseling that may take place in a church or parish but also for pastors who represent religious communities as institutional or military chaplains.

The pastor's wisdom is relational when it conveys a sense of security to the person who is sharing some of his life with the pastor. It is relational when it is "care-full" and sensitive to the feelings of the persons with whom he is in conversation. It is relational when it is an honest and genuine expression of who the pastor is as a person, not just something he thinks he ought to say. Obviously not all ministers possess this wisdom to the same degree, but it is something that can be further developed by attention to and learning from their relationships with persons in the institutions or religious communities in which they serve and to which they are responsible.

Relational wisdom contributes to what in institutional chaplaincy is often called spiritual care, but it clearly grows out of the faith and images of the Christian tradition. It is based on faith in a relational God who is present in human relationships with the shepherd's care for both the whole flock of sheep and for the individual one or two who, for some reason, are separated from the supportive experience of the group.

The Meanings of *Pastoral*

The term *pastoral* may be less familiar today for people who have lived primarily in an urban rather than a rural setting. Moreover, the common understanding of the pastoral relationship as growing out of a dominant and submissive relationship between shepherds and sheep has in recent years contributed to a negative understanding of the pastoral image. This book attempts to correct or modify that negative image by asserting both of the two important meanings of the term *pastoral*. As the pastoral image from Luke's Gospel suggests, the pastor may be called to find and care for one lost sheep, but that part of the story is told against the backdrop of the shepherd leaving the flock to do that. The power of the story depends on the tension of the two responsibilities and the fact that the majority of the pastor's task is caring for a spirited flock that is not lost. Both meanings of *pastor* are essential for understanding the image and applying it to the pastoral care of persons.

The meaning of pastor as keeper of the whole flock is similar to the New Testament meaning of *bishop*. A pastor is like a shepherd in that he has oversight, supervisory, or administrative responsibility for a whole group, whether one is speaking of sheep or persons. In some traditions, in churches where there is more than one minister, it is only the senior minister who is understood to be the pastor. He is the one thought to have sufficient wisdom and experience to be the supervisor, and usually it is the public and supervisory part of his work where the pastor develops his reputation and through which most people know him.

The second meaning of *pastor* comes particularly from its association with the image in Luke 15 of a shepherd going in search of the lost sheep, even at the risk of limiting his time to care for the whole flock. Although this image is far less familiar than it once was, most any news program on television today presents at least one story of loss or separation. We continue to be inspired today by stories of those who are willing to go after persons and things that are lost in spite of the risk that the effort may involve. And most of us are aware of different kinds of lostness, including the lostness that we describe in this book, the lostness or separation from families and communities of care.

Shepherd is much more an image of personal strength than one of dominance over lesser creatures. The pastor, who is like the shepherd, risks failing to fulfill his broader responsibilities in order to go after one or two who are lost. The strength necessary to take this risk is an important part of the meaning of *shepherd* in the story. Being a pastor is having enough wisdom and strength to deal with this kind of tension between two often-conflicted functional roles. The concern for lostness in tension with overall pastoral or supervisory responsibility for a faith community is the continuing meaning of the term *pastoral* today.

Counseling is a natural part of the pastoral care that the religious community or institution offers; therefore, parish ministers or chaplains who serve outside a religious community provide counseling as an extension of their pastoral care. Such counseling is not a private practice, something done apart from the regular ministry of the community the minister represents. It is important, therefore, that the group within the religious community to which the minister is accountable know about and support the counseling that is done as a part of the pastor's or chaplain's pastoral care. And as a part of this understanding and support they need to be aware of how much counseling the pastor does and be able to consult with him about limiting or extending the counseling done as a part of the pastor's ministry. More discussion about limits will be found in the next chapter.

What a Pastor Is Expected to Have

In quite a number of religious communities the traditional words used for giving authority in the ordination of clergy are something like this: "Take thou Authority to preach the Word of God, and to administer the holy Sacraments in the Congregation." That statement can be understood broadly or quite narrowly. We are speaking in this chapter of how a minister who has taken that authority symbolically can actually express it in his ministry. With respect to conducting and certifying marriages, the state confirms the authority given to the pastor by the religious body of which he is a part. Pastors themselves need to have a sense of the relevance of the authority given to them for the lives of persons so that in difficult life situations they are not so anxious about making a mistake that they cannot be fully present with those who need their help. Some of that authority is conveyed in more formal and objective ways through his ordination as a minister and by the academic degrees he may hold. More of it, however, rests in the way he functions, in his representation of the values of a community of faith and of what life ought to be, as well as in what he himself is expected to be as a person.

4

In a discussion of pastoral counseling as an extension of pastoral care, consideration of the meaning of *pastoral authority* is a helpful counterpoint to the common association of pastoral care with a passive or reactive understanding of ministry as expressed primarily through listening. Seeing pastoral care as essentially passive care contrasts with a more assertive view of ministry that takes place in preaching, teaching, and administering the programs of an organization. Actually "care-full" listening is not passive. It is quite active and often interruptive in order to gain a genuine understanding of person and problem.

Pastoral authority used in pastoral counseling, as well as in other functions of ministry, is an expression of both a profession and a calling. Christian ethicist James Gustafson said that,

> A "calling" without professionalization is bumbling, ineffective and even dangerous. A profession without a calling, however, has no taps of moral and human rootage to keep motivation alive, to keep human sensitivities and sensibilities alert, and to nourish a proper sense of self-fulfillment. Nor does a professional without a calling easily envision the larger ends and purposes of human good that our individual efforts can serve. (James M. Gustafson, "Professions as Callings," *Social Service Review*, December 1982, 514)

Although the expression of pastoral authority may involve the use of any management and communication skills that the minister acquires, the theological assertion that the practice of ministry is a calling affirms that the use of those skills cannot appropriately be used apart from the community of faith authorizing them and the person of the minister using them. Thus counseling done by a parish minister or institutional chaplain is not a private practice. It is an action of the faith community that the minister performs on the community's behalf.

Some other things about the expression of pastoral authority in pastoral counseling should be said here. The first is that it is not based upon what the pastor says or does but upon supporting and encouraging the counselee in making choices and changes in his own life. Change is frightening to most people whether or not they can admit it. The pastor's authority is expressed in his willingness to be present in change and transitions

5

in life and, when judged to be appropriate, to bless those changes and transitions.

A second thing to be said is that expressing pastoral authority involves risk to the pastor's self. In some ways this risk is parallel to the risk of the counselee in making choices and changes in his life situation. In attempting to guide another, the pastor may be wrong in some of what he says, but if that guidance is given with the honesty of self-expression it has more likelihood of offering positive guidance than hiddenness and ambiguity in what is said. The counselee will have more sense that the pastor is *there*, and the pastor's own self-expression can encourage that of the person seeking help.

A third element in the expression of pastoral authority is that it is not just based on words. Again, it is presence, being there with the faith that the pastor represents. It may involve ritual such as the structure the pastor uses for the counseling or a blessing or informal touch. It may involve, if this is not just words but something the pastor honestly does, telling the counselee that he prays for him in this time of change or transition. Certainly prayer involves words, but these words reference a ritual behavior that is taking place outside the actual counseling. The beyond words behavior that can express the pastor's authority may, for example, also be expressed by his not telling the counselee to come back for further counseling but insisting that he make the decision about that himself.

Something that is negatively related to all the characteristics noted above is the need to please, to be "nice," to have difficulty saying "no." The pastor asserts his authority in insisting on conducting the counseling in the way he thinks best, and this sometimes involves saying "no" to the way the counselee wants to proceed. More will be said about this, particularly in the discussion of pastoral counseling related to problems of addiction and abuse.

What a Pastor Is Expected to Be

Although we may live in a time in the United States when church and ministry are less influential than they seem to have been in the past, many persons still look to pastors for help with personal and family problems.

They come to pastors for counseling because the pastor appears to be more available and less threatening than psychotherapists who may be identified as only treating those who are thought of as mentally ill.

Like the good physician, a pastor is expected to be a certain kind of person. The religious body that ordains the pastor and the person who comes to him for counseling don't have to agree on what this specialness about him should be. Some of it is that he is expected to be an educated professional with special knowledge and convictions about life and how it should be lived. Some of it is related to the faith of the religious tradition that the pastor represents.

Within the Christian tradition an important example of how the New Testament, particularly the later epistles, understood what a pastor should be is found in 1 Timothy 3:1-7. Wayne Oates referenced this text in his classic book *The Christian Pastor*. I paraphrased that same text thirty years later in my book *Pastoral Care in Context* in chapter 3, "Characteristics of the Carers," (Louisville: Westminster/John Knox, 1993). The text in 1 Timothy is describing what bishops should be. *The Common English Bible* translates the Greek word for bishop, *episkopos*, as supervisor, and this touches on one of the meanings of the word *pastor* that I commented on previously.

> [Pastors or] the church's supervisors must be without fault. They should be faithful to their spouse, sober, modest, and honest. They should show hospitality and be skilled at teaching. They should not be addicted to alcohol or be a bully. Instead, they should be gentle, peaceable, and not greedy. They should manage their own household well—they should see that their children are obedient with complete respect, because if they don't know how to manage their own household, how can they take care of God's church? They shouldn't be new believers so that they won't become proud and fall under the devil's spell. They should also have a good reputation with those outside the church so that they won't be embarrassed and fall into the devil's trap. (1 Tim 3:2-7 CEB)

How might we understand these expectations today? My current interpretation of the text is given below. My way of putting this is not important, but it is intended to say that it is important for ministers to take seriously how they are viewed by church and community. This does not mean uniformity of behavior, but it does mean that what they do in ministry cannot be separated from the persons they are. They should not be naive about or indifferent to the facts and affirmations of the faith. Uniformity in their theological education is not required, but serious involvement in such education is.

Pastors should also be aware of how their relationship to their own families may affect the way they approach and respond to the pain in the families of other persons. The minister's own marital status is not as important as his awareness of the importance of issues of intimacy and closeness in the lives of everyone. Such issues cannot be separated from more explicitly "religious" concerns. At the same time it is important that ministers be able to handle personal issues with objectivity and wisdom, not using the situation of others to work on their own personal concerns.

Ministers should be committed to the importance of faith for their own lives. Their convictions cannot afford to be casual. They must be firmly but not defensively held in a way that they are available for dialogue, not indoctrination. Pastors' attitude about their ministry is important. They obviously cannot be happy about all the tasks of ministry, but they should have a way of doing them that is not resentful and hostile about having to do the work.

These statements about what ministers should be and do may not be in the awareness of those who come to them for counsel, but they are useful reminders that representatives and leaders of religious communities are expected in some way to have a special knowledge and ability as well as an association with a profession representing a worthwhile or more meaningful life. Thus in their counseling, pastors need to embody and be seeking to embody in a more profound way an understanding of life and of meaningful relationships.

What a Pastor Is Supposed to Do

In addition to the term *pastoral*, the meanings of *counsel, counseling,* and *pastoral consultation* are important in describing the kind of counseling the pastor should do with persons seeking help. *Counsel* is a term that most often is associated with the legal profession. It is commonly understood as advice, opinion, or instruction given in directing the judgment or conduct of another. Other understandings of *counsel* include the interchange of opinions as to future procedure; consultation; deliberation; a deliberate purpose; plan; design; and in theology, as one of the advisory declarations of Christ. All of these ways of describing *counsel* can be useful in thinking about the care that a minister who is not a counseling specialist can give.

The terms *counseling* and *psychotherapy* are often used interchangeably, but a common distinction between the two is that counseling is more often associated with thoughtful reflection and decision about a person's life situation, whereas psychotherapy is more concerned with personality change and improved mental health. Psychotherapy is usually a longer-term process requiring more psychological knowledge and technical skill on the part of the therapist. Counseling is likely to be a short-term, more cognitively focused process. Although pastors who do not intend to specialize in counseling can profit from some study of the techniques of psychotherapy and from being patients in psychotherapy themselves, they can generally be more effective if they consider themselves as counselors who focus more on a person's dealing with his life situation than on personal, psychological change. One qualification to this statement is that religious change, often described as conversion and guided by a pastor in ministry both to the whole community and to individual persons, may indeed involve significant psychological change. The focus of the pastor's counsel of individuals and families, however, is usually on issues of personal change that can be discussed cognitively.

Other words associated with the dictionary definitions of *counsel* and *counseling* noted above were *consultation, deliberation, deliberate purpose, plan,* and *design.* And specifically related to theology, counseling related for the aid of living morally and achieving a good and moral life. All of them are associated with the meaning of advice and the achieving of a more satisfying life whether or not one that is in some way thought of as perfect. A minister or religious leader is generally thought of as a consultant on what a good life is, whether or not the person consulting

Cruseel V.
Supervisor

with him is particularly concerned with values that are specifically Christian.

Because we are describing the minister's role and function as a counselor or consultant it seems important to say something about what I understand as the meaning of those terms for pastoral counseling. Consultation is generally understood by contrasting it to supervision. A supervisor is a person who is responsible for the completion of a task that another person is carrying out. If the work is not done effectively, the supervisor as well as the person supervised may suffer the consequences of that failure. Consultation is different in that the consultant, unlike the supervisor, is not responsible for what the person consulted does or thinks. He simply examines the situation as an experienced and knowledgeable person. He gives his opinion on or response to the situation, and the person or persons consulted are free to take or leave what has been given them.

Consultation extends beyond this more general understanding to the situation of a minister who offers counsel or consultation to persons about their lives. In the *Dictionary of Pastoral Care and Counseling* ([Nashville: Abingdon Press, 1990] 223-224), which I paraphrase here, O. L. DeLozier observes that, except for the most dependent relationships of childhood, and in some conditions of being a patient, no one knows what is best for another person. Recognizing this frees us from the burdensome task of knowing what is best for another. The consultant, therefore, is able to be open enough as a person to offer a variety of responses and impressions with the confidence that the person consulted can pick and choose what is useful. I believe that is something very important for pastors to consider when they are called upon to give advice in either the language of theology or the language of everyday life.

Wisdom as Slowing Down

The kind of counseling that a pastor can most effectively do requires using the wisdom about life and relationships that he has developed through responding with pastoral care to particular situations of human lostness. Moreover, pastors can appropriately be expected to continue developing wisdom about relationships through disciplined reflection upon their pastoral experience. Before going on to describe this relational kind of wisdom, however, it seems important to discuss some of the ways that wisdom has been understood in everyday life situations.

Most commonly, wisdom is viewed as the ability to make sound choices and good decisions in the midst of life's complications. It is something that comes from making mistakes and learning from them; it is not something a person is born with. A person who has wisdom has often been understood as one who can maintain a larger view of the situation to be addressed without losing sight of the particularity and the intricacies of interrelationships within that situation. It involves an assumption that life situations are almost always complex and defy quick solutions.

Because of the complexity of so many human situations that pastors have to deal with, wisdom almost always involves slowing down the demand that something must be done immediately. Wisdom insists that thinking take place before doing something to "fix" the problem. Wisdom is in this sense something that a pastor needs in order to allow the slow-down process to take place. It is also something that a pastoral relationship can make possible because of its usually calming, supportive nature. Certainly there are genuine emergency situations or problems where action needs to be taken at once, but most situations that are presented as emergencies to helping persons really aren't that, and a pastor's wisdom is first expressed by trying to slow things down. Wisdom usually is more effectively offered not by doing but by waiting and thinking about what should be done.

Wisdom is about slowing down and thinking before acting; it is supported by the wisdom literature in the Bible—Proverbs, Job, and Ecclesiastes. These books, like pastoral care and counseling, are most often dealing with practical life concerns that are not, when first presented, specifically religious. In contrast with much of the Bible, Proverbs, like pastoral care and counseling, is not as concerned with unfolding the salvation story of God and humankind. These books seem to assume that story and deal with understanding and responding to the ordinary situations of human life.

Proverbs, particularly, seems to address the question, "If we really are God's people, how should we live our lives?" Probably the most important likeness between the biblical proverbs and the kind of counseling that pastors need to do is that neither of them offers commandments that tell you what to do. Rather, by and large they present pointed statements designed to help you think before you act rather than simply reacting to what's said or done. Similar to the book of Proverbs, the practice of pastoral care and counseling simply assumes the faith story and goes on to respond to those problems of life that usually are not expressed in explicitly religious language. At times pastoral counselors may refer to some things in the Bible's salvation story, but only occasionally does the value of what they do in a counseling conversation rest upon telling that story again.

The book of Proverbs is also similar to pastoral care and counseling in that rather than calling for the constant use religious language, it directs pastors to pay attention to deeper meanings in the ordinary language of life, assuming that a relationship with God or a dimension of spirituality is a part of a person's life whether God or the practice of religion is spoken of or not. This makes me think of what I heard many times from patients when I was a hospital chaplain: "Remember me, Reverend." When these words came from persons who had little or no experience or interest in talking about prayer or directly requesting it. The pastor's wisdom involves the availability to talk seriously about life and its meaning without needing to talk explicitly about God.

Wisdom and Guidance

The meaning of the word *guidance* is strongly associated with the meaning of *wisdom*. It is commonly understood as something offered to others regarding a course of action that should be taken. The word *guidance* is derived from a historically earlier word that means to observe; it can also mean going before and going with or in some fashion showing the way. Pastoral guidance is like that, but it is also significantly different. It is more related to the presence of the guide and the relationship offered than to a specific course that the guide suggests. Guidance that can be understood as pastoral care is not guidance relevant for all or most people but something that may be very relevant and useful to a particular person or small group.

To return to images of the care of the flock and care for the lost sheep, the guidance necessary for the whole flock is seldom the guidance that is most helpful in enabling the lost or separated sheep overcome lostness. Genuine pastoral guidance is developed out of understanding in-depth the predicament of the particular person separated by present circumstances from the larger group. The pastor should balance use of any knowledge he feels may contribute to guiding another with the awareness that it is the counselee who knows the most about the kind of guidance needed.

It seems important to remind the pastor here that the most ineffective guidance he can offer is some version of "Everything is going to be all right," particularly when that or something like it is said without full attention having been given to the problem presented. Although that message ultimately may be accurate, it is too often given without facts to base that message upon. Such generalized reassurance is usually a means of dealing with the pastor's own anxiety in not quite knowing what to say or do. Reassurance that can contribute to effective pastoral guidance is based on specific positive changes that the pastor has noticed and that the parishioner can confirm.

Pastoral guidance is not directing the person's life but reminding that person of specific resources that have been part of his life, though they may now be absent or weak. Guiding involves listening for the whole story; telling the person something of what has been heard; and reminding him that the illness, the grief, the broken relationship he is experiencing now is not all that there is to him and his life. The authority used in guidance is based on pastoral presence and "care-full" listening.

Wisdom as Vision and Discernment

Charles Wood writes about the kind of wisdom that theological education should produce (*Vision and Discernment* [Atlanta: Scholars Press, 1985], 57–77). Wood describes such wisdom in terms of vision and discernment. Vision, he says, is a grasp of things in their wholeness and their relatedness—how things hang together. The word *discernment* comes from the Latin *discernere*, meaning to sift through. Discernment is the counter-point to vision and may be thought of as insight into specific situations in their particularity.

An important part of both vision and discernment is developing the capacity for listening carefully. As I have described it in another place: Listening is not just a matter of using one's ears and hearing words. It is a total response to the way that the carer is experiencing the other person. A useful guide for this can be found in Luke 8:18, which the New Revised Standard Version translates "pay attention to how you listen."

> *Blepete* literally means "see"—"see how you listen." The Greek word denotes sense perception or being able to see as distinct from blindness. It seems to call on all the senses for full awareness of the message being conveyed. (Patton, *Pastoral Care in Context*, 214; the original text pointed the reader to see Kittel's *Theolgoical Dictionary of the New Testament*, ed. Gerhard Kittel, trans. and ed. Geoffrey W. Bromiley, vol. 5 [Grand Rapids: Wm. B. Eerdmans Publishing Co., 1967], 343–50)

The text challenges us to be "care-full" in the way that we listen and to try to remember what we hear.

Discernment can also be understood as an intuitive process that is similar to the recognition of a long-lost friend. It can apply both to the recognition of another and the recognition of something in oneself. Much about the friend and about oneself may have changed. The outer appearance is almost completely different from the way he was, but there is some inner something about the person that is recognizable as one I knew and still know.

In John's Gospel picture of Jesus, he is one who discerns the mark of a particular kind of character in persons that may not be obvious to others. He sees Nathaniel as a "genuine Israelite in whom there is no deceit" (John 1:47 CEB). He calls disciples to follow him who appear on the surface to be quite ordinary. Discernment also has some of the character of Paul's description in 2 Corinthians 2:14-16 of the Christians having a distinctive aroma. The identifying mark is discerned in a more primitive way that the higher senses of seeing and hearing cannot perceive.

Discernment is the process that allows pastors who counsel to focus deeply upon the life and concerns of another person. Because in their formation as ministers, pastors themselves have in some significant way been discerned and known; they have a foundation for being able to discern and know others in their counsel of them. More important, because we believe that God remembers and has discerned us, we can remember other persons in our care of them. Because we have been valued, we can value others as we hear and remember them through the agency of our wisdom.

There is an interesting and perhaps informative parallel between wisdom understood as involving both vision and discernment and the two meanings of *pastoral* that were discussed earlier—the oversight of the whole and care for the particular. A wise pastor is one who possesses both a vision of the whole and discernment of the particular and whose vision and discernment informs his practice and is in turn informed by it.

Meanings of *Relationality*

Relational wisdom involves an increasing ability to participate fully in relationships, being able to learn from them, and being able to discuss them with persons to whom the pastor is offering counseling and from whom he is asking consultation. Essential for such relational thinking is a view of human being that grows out of the religious tradition that the pastor represents and a psychological understanding that is more concerned with the whole person in relationship than specific behaviors or thinking. The modern era of pastoral care education began with the holistic theories of personality first published in the late 1930s. In the 1950s and 1960s, these earlier views were broadened to include thinking of persons more in terms of their interpersonal relationships and their membership in family systems. The relational wisdom that is the pastor's specialty is informed both by some of these psychological theories of the person and by the Christian tradition that the minister represents, namely, that humankind was created for relationship with God and other human beings. To persons who live in a web of relationships, the minister can be a reminder of that tradition and belief. Pastors are called to be present with persons in need in order to use their relational wisdom to sort out what needs to be said and done within those relationships.

Postmodern and culturally informed thinking has warned us about developing norms for human relationality (or norms for anything else) that come primarily from one culture, one race, one gender or any other singular influencing factor. We have learned to attend to the particulars in any situation and to avoid generalizations about it based on an unacknowledged perspective of our own. In recent years, pastors have been influenced in their caring by what I have called the communal-contextual paradigm for pastoral care and its critique of individualistic and unicultural thinking and acting. Nevertheless, in all their many culturally and gender-conditioned different ways, I believe that human beings are relational, and the pastor can be a reminder of this and, for many people, a specialist in consulting with persons about these relationships.

I'm not concerned to argue for any one psychological theory for developing and maintaining relational wisdom, but reading, studying, and reflecting on ministry should continually be informed by sound relational theory that includes ethical and theological understandings of relationships, family studies, group theory, and system and organizational theory. I offer here only a few examples of several theories that have been helpful to me during my years as a pastoral carer and counselor. The pastor who is concerned to develop his relational wisdom should make use of any of these and of other relational theories that seem more helpful to him.

A strongly relational theorist that was particularly helpful to me early in my work and one who continues to be useful today is Harry Stack Sullivan. He was a psychiatrist who wrote with an obscure kind of terminology that has not been used by later relational theorists, but most of them were in some way influenced by his theories. Sullivan's early work was with deeply disturbed mental hospital patients and has some similarity to that of Anton Boisen, the founder of clinical pastoral education. Both of them affirmed the humanity of the patients whose illness made them seem so different from others. Sullivan did this with what he called his one genus hypothesis, that "We are all more alike than otherwise." In his relational wisdom there was an affirmation of the ordinary humanity of the patient.

In contrast to his use in this instance of the ordinary language of life, Sullivan's characterization of what a helping person should be was the rather abstract-sounding term "expert in interpersonal relations." However, whatever the level of expertness the person is able to achieve I think this term is close in meaning to what I have described as "relational wisdom." Although one might hesitate to apply the term *expert* to many pastors, they are constantly involved in interpersonal relationships and challenged to develop their ability to deal effectively with them.

Following Sullivan, the interpersonal expert should first of all be extraordinarily perceptive in responding to anxiety and noticing the detail of the kind of anxiety involved in relationships. Second, he needs to offer enough security to the other person to allow him to talk about what he needs, thus enabling understanding of his immediate situation and his life as a whole. Sullivan described the third characteristic of the interpersonal expert as "realness." He should be genuine—as honest as possible without offering a threatening critique of the other. The expert's relationships and communication should be simple, direct, and practical. Having dealt with terribly anxious persons who confused their speech in order to deal with their anxiety, Sullivan sought to be present with his patients in a down-to-earth, simple, and understandable way. I believe that the pastor's relational wisdom should be exhibited in a similar simple way and that simplicity can contribute to his ability to offer trusted relationships.

In addition to Sullivan's theoretical contribution to relational wisdom, what I believe can be most helpful to a pastor is the awareness of and continuing study of the three fundamental human relationships that grow out of the experience of being a family member. These same types of relationships are present not only in the family but in virtually all areas of life. They are relationships (1) with authorities such as parents, (2) with peers like brothers and sisters or friends, and (3) with persons to whom one is himself is an authority or parent-like figure. 4. Self

In a previous writing about the family I have discussed these kinds of relationships by insisting that a Christian family is best identified not by the form in which it exists but by the way its members care for their generations: the generation before them, their parental generation; their own generation, composed of brothers and sisters and other peers; and the generation that comes after them, their children or younger or less-experienced persons for whom they care. Being relationally wise requires that we pay attention to and continue to learn about all three of these relationships. Parenthetically, I believe that much of the strength of clinical pastoral education has been its constant examination of those relationships in the process of supervising ministry.

Many of us assume that our relationships with authorities are the most difficult to deal with, but it is important for the counselee himself and the one who offers counsel to him to examine all three types of relationships and see how they are interrelated. How is the staff member with whom the pastor is consulting dealing with his peers, with his patients, with his supervisors, and how is that related to his life experience insofar as that is available to the pastor and him? If we learn to think about and explore these three relationships for ourselves and for others, we can continually contribute to our competence in the specialty of relational wisdom.

In addition to developing sensitivity, security, and realness in relationship and in paying significant attention to the three basic types of life relationships, relational wisdom also requires having a theory about groups that guides pastors both in their participation in and leadership of groups and in their consultation with individuals and families. Group theory and practice is something that continually needs to be developed through study and experience. There are many valuable theories about participating in and leading groups. The theories that have been most helpful to me are those that have emphasized that groups have two essential needs: (1) accomplishing a task and (2) satisfying the personal or emotional needs of the group members. A group and its leader need to achieve a practical balance between accomplishing a task and meeting the group's emotional needs, such as needs for recognition and relationship. Furthermore, it is important to be aware of the way the two needs are being expressed by the group as a whole, its individual members, and by the group leader. It is essential for the pastor who counsels to work with an effective group theory and practice it in the development of his relational wisdom.

Summary

This chapter begins with a discussion of some of the reasons that persons come to ministers for counseling. It is noted that ministers seem more available and less threatening to many people than mental health professionals. Perhaps more important is that ministers often represent a wisdom about a good life and its meaning even for persons who are not members of religious communities.

The major concern of the chapter, however, is about the meaning of the relational wisdom that a pastor may be able to offer through his counseling. Much of this wisdom grows out of what a pastor represents, namely a God who remembers and cares about us and our life situations and a religious community that attempts to live out God's caring in practical ways. The term *pastoral* represents the care that the stories of loss in Luke 15 present. The meaning of *pastoral* is relevant today in nonrural settings because we continue to be concerned for the care of those who are some way lost or separated from what is more important to them.

Relational wisdom is discussed as a kind of practical approach to life that involves thinking about the troubling situation of the person or persons seeking help. It is further characterized as a slowing down and a time to think carefully about the situation before acting or encouraging the counselee to act. The purpose of this slowing is to enable the troubled person to use the presence and support of the pastor to deal more effectively with the experience of loss or separation. What this wisdom involves is described in terms of vision and discernment, careful ways of seeing both the larger situation and the important details of it.

Finally, some of the things that define wisdom as relational are discussed as characteristics that the minister needs to have and needs to be working to develop in order to do effective counseling. These relational qualities are described as sensitivity to the person's feelings about his situation, an ability to offer security and a sense of safeness in spite of the problem, and a realness and honesty in reacting to it. There is also a discussion of how the three basic life relationships are being dealt with: with authorities; with peers; and with those to whom the person himself is an authority, such as a teacher or parent. Finally, there is a brief discussion of group relationships, as a member and a leader, and some ways of thinking about what the needs of a group are.

Although ministers who offer pastoral counsel may not possess wisdom understood in this relational way, it is important and possible for them to be working toward developing it. Fortunately, because of what they may represent to persons seeking help, this effort may be enough to allow them to have some effectiveness in their counsel, whatever the level of their experience. The next chapter begins the discussion of the way relational wisdom can be used in offering pastoral counseling.

Chapter Two

The First Pastoral Counseling Conversation

Reading a book that tells you how to do things is not sufficient for learning how to be a counselor. Face-to-face supervision or consultation on your work with an experienced supervisor is where genuine dialogue can take place. The suggestions presented here about a way of conducting the counseling conversation engage the pastoral reader in a dialogue about the things that need to take place, particularly in a first meeting. I cannot know the reader's response to my suggestions, but having had many actual conversations with students and pastors about these matters, I believe my suggestions regarding what one needs to think about and do in order to conduct an effective meeting for counseling can be valuable and useful.

The pastor should enter into counseling remembering that it's like pastoral care, but it's different. It's like the pastoral care that she knows something about and can make use of in the counseling. On the other hand, it's different. It requires a definite plan and a structure for some of the things that should happen in the meeting. The practical purpose of the first meeting is to arrive at an initial understanding of the person or persons who have come, the problem they present, and further development of the relationship they have with the pastor and the religious community that pastor represents.

Another important thing to remember is that what pastors who counsel can offer to persons who ask to meet with them is relationship with a person who represents maturity in the faith and who has or is developing the emotional capacity to be a parent. Whatever the chronological age, pastoral counselors need to be emotionally and spiritually "middle-aged," having the capacity to facilitate the development of another rather than needing to do something to prove their own adequacy. They can be personally available in the counseling process because they have most of their personal needs met in other relationships. The pastor's style of conversation should offer the counselee a good example of what it means to be a mature human being.

Securing Understanding and Support for the Pastor's Counseling Ministry

Before engaging in pastoral counseling, particularly in a new setting for ministry, it is important for the pastor to clarify with a committee to which she is responsible the way in which pastoral counseling may be a part of her ministry. This can be done as a part of clarifying the pastor's job description so that the pastor and the committee have a common understanding of the way she understands her job and how she plans to use her time. Part of that general discussion involves the way pastoral care will be carried out and how pastoral counseling may be a part of that. The pastor should indicate that her pastoral counseling will be limited to a few meetings with those who seek help from her and that referral to a more specialized mental health professional may be a part of her counseling ministry. The pastor and those to whom she is responsible should both be aware that a significant part of her pastor's counseling ministry can be an effective referral to a more specialized professional helper. And that referral is much more likely to be effective if it takes place after a meeting with a caring pastor. An important part of the pastor's calling is to respond to a person's need and request for help and also to prepare the way for persons to receive help from others.

Within the context of this discussion of pastoral care and counseling it is important to say that a pastor, particularly one who is new to a community, needs to get to know the competent professional persons to whom she might refer. In getting to know the members of a church or the staff of an institution, the pastor listens to hear about persons who have been helpful to them in difficult situations. She is concerned to hear about effective mental health counselors, physicians, attorneys, and other helping persons or agencies. Then, as soon as reasonable, the pastor should call or try to visit with some of them in order to develop some more direct, personal knowledge of them. Referrals are much more likely to be effective if the pastor can refer to a professional person whom she actually knows. A referral to a known person is almost always more effective than simply making a referral to an agency. And again, counseling with a mental health professional is more likely be effective if the person referred has already had a helpful relationship with someone like a pastor.

The First Conversation about Counseling

Pastoral counseling begins with the first conversation suggesting that the person with whom the pastor is conversing is aware of some need for help. The conversation is not just about setting up a meeting for counseling. It is the actual beginning of the counseling relationship, and it offers the opportunity to make the person seeking help more comfortable about being in the position of asking for help. Precounseling conversations can have that value even if no meeting for counseling is ever scheduled. In these conversations, the pastor can be identified as someone who seems to be understanding and available for help should the person want to consult with her later or just gain some satisfaction from the fact that a person like the pastor is there.

The conversations may take place over the telephone, in the hallway of the church, at the end of a class or other group meeting, or most any other circumstance. It is usually a type of informal pastoral care that happens before any meeting for counseling is set, and there may be several brief conversations through which the seeking person is assessing whether or not the pastor seems to be a trustworthy person with whom one can share one's deeper concerns or pain. As we noted in the introduction to this book, one of the advantages that seeing a pastor has over many other helping professionals is that she may be more available for these exploratory encounters before any arrangement for counseling takes place. And these informal, friendly meetings can pave the way for more significant meetings in any counseling that takes place later on.

To develop the relational wisdom needed for counseling, the pastor pays attention to what is said in the first conversations with a person who may later come for pastoral counseling. That person may be assessing whether or not the pastor seems like the kind of person who may offer some wisdom about the larger and more painful concerns in life. If the first conversation takes place over the telephone, it may be a more direct request for counsel or one in which the person discusses a less personal issue related to something about the church and then mentions that he would also like to talk about something else. The point of this discussion of precounseling conversations is to encourage the pastor to see them as a part of the counseling relationship and to urge the pastor to think of them as guides for any later relationship.

Thinking about and Planning the Counseling before It Takes Place

Thinking about and planning how the counseling might develop begins before the very first meeting with the person seeking help, and it should continue throughout any counseling that does take place. Such thinking is a major part of the pastor's developing wisdom. Some of that early or preliminary thinking and planning has to do with who should be present in the meeting for counseling. Should it take place with only the person who first contacted the pastor present, or should other concerned members of the family be involved? If the reason for counseling appears to be a problem with marriage, the pastor should suggest that the marital partners might come together to the counseling session. Having the appropriate persons involved in the counseling process is often more important than what is said in their meeting.

24

If the first contact with the person seeking counsel is someone whom the pastor does not know, it is appropriate and important for the pastor to ask about how that person happened to call her. That may give some understanding about what the person is looking for. If the person calling was referred by someone the pastor knows, that can also offer clues about how any counseling relationship may develop. The pastor might say something like this, "Can you tell me briefly about why you decided to contact me?" If the caller speaks of an issue related to the family, then it is helpful to ask about any others who are a part of the caller's household and whether one or more of them might want to be involved in the meeting with the pastor. Doing this suggests that the pastor is concerned with the relationships that may form the context for the counseling.

As a part of the pastor's thinking about what to do in the counseling, there are two important things to keep in mind. The first is something that has been already emphasized several times earlier in this book, that what the pastor is doing in counseling is an extension of what she already knows something about: pastoral care. The pastor's knowledge and experience as a pastoral carer in crisis times in the parish or a hospital will help her in offering counsel whatever the presenting problem in the counseling may be. The pastor does not need to know a great deal about the problem that the counselee presents. In most cases, the person who comes to her for counseling has enough knowledge to deal with the problem. What he usually needs, therefore, is a context (relationship) within which the resources necessary to deal with the problem can be mobilized. What pastoral counseling offers is a supportive relationship with a professional person who represents hope for a good and more meaningful life and who is disciplined and honest in her caring for persons.

The second thing to keep in mind in thinking about a first counseling conversation is that a plan for what is going to happen is needed. This does not mean that the pastor is going to control or dominate the meeting. It simply means that she is going to conduct the counseling as if she knows what she is doing because she has a plan for it. A general principle for meetings between two or more persons is that the less training and experience the leader (in this case the pastor) has, the more structure or plan she needs for conducting the meeting. This need for structure may be thought of as a counterpoint to other types of pastoral care where the pastor may have learned primarily to listen and simply respond to what has been expressed in the conversation. In pastoral care the reason for the meeting is at least initially clear. In pastoral counseling it needs to be clarified, and that is what planning and structuring can offer the counseling relationship.

As in other aspects of the pastor's pastoral care ministry, what she is doing in counseling involves listening "care-fully." Adding the suffix "full" to *care* indicates that thinking about how one's care is being expressed is a significant part of the caring process. In one sense it is a natural process and should be what the pastor is honestly feeling, but it involves serious thinking about what one is hearing and how to respond now and later. The care can be "full" when it involves feelings, thoughts, and actions and, insofar as possible, all of the senses. It should also be said that it requires self-awareness as well as awareness of the other in order to do this. The pastor needs to ask herself, "How am I feeling in this conversation, and how do I seem to be coming across to this person as we talk about him and his problems?"

The "care-full" listening that takes place in pastoral care occurs because the pastor or members of the religious community have decided that a particular person is in some way lost or separated from what is important to him and needs some help in order to be reconnected. The initiative for care comes from the caring community and those who take action to express that. In pastoral counseling the person needing help takes the action necessary to get a pastoral response by letting the pastor or someone associated with her know that he is looking for someone to help with a problem. All that the pastor has learned about listening in pastoral care should go on in the meeting for counseling, but in a counseling conversation more of a plan is needed in order for the pastor and the person seeking help not to get lost in the details of what the troubled person is expressing.

Without having some plan in mind for what needs to take place in the meeting, it is difficult to keep track of what pastor and counselee need to be working on together, and they will have no idea what to do or say when the conversation stops abruptly. Although experienced psychotherapists can often make good use of long silences, inexperienced pastoral counselors seldom can, particularly in a first meeting for counseling. The pastor needs to give the person seeking help an opportunity to ventilate his concerns and thereby reduce the anxiety associated with them. In order to understand how those concerns might best be dealt with, however, a plan or structure is needed to help understand what is presented in a way that the pastor can be fully in touch with it. That structure involves an evaluation of the person and the problem so that both pastor and counselee can both have some common understanding of what's going on.

Just as a pastor in a sermon on a biblical text attempts to put the text in the context of the whole book that it comes from and the time and situation in history that the text was addressing, the pastor tries to do a similar thing with the counselee's problem. She should not think about the problem apart from a broader understanding of the person presenting it. Sufficient interest in the problem and how it is being experienced is important in that the person asking for help is not usually aware of asking for help with his whole life. Nevertheless, one of the major purposes of the evaluative structure is putting the problem in context and, sometimes more important, opening up the opportunity of a larger dialogue about the person's life, values, and goals. The structure can also encourage the counselee to see the problem presented as being both external to him and, at the same time, also a part of the way he is—internal to him as well as external.

How to Begin the First Meeting

One of the most helpful ways for a pastor to begin a counseling conversation is to speak briefly about what preceded it, particularly how she understands why they got together. For example,

> You called me on the phone last Wednesday and indicated that it might be helpful for us to get together. I believe that you mentioned that it had something to do with an uncomfortable encounter you had with your supervisor at work, but I don't remember any more of what you said about that. There

may be some other things that we need to talk about, but that's all that I know now about our getting together today. I don't know how much time we'll need to talk about this. I have an hour now before I have another commitment, and I can certainly schedule some more time if we need to.

The advantage of this kind of beginning is that it takes the pressure off the help seeker to quickly explain why he's there and lets him know that the pastor is already taking his concerns seriously. The pastor tries to convey that she is responding only to what she has heard from the person she is with and does not bring in anything she may have heard about this person's concerns from any other source. It begins the process of the pastor's openness in telling the other person what she has heard and something of what she does not know and may need to know about. At this time she should also convey how much time she has available now for their counseling conversation.

At that point the pastor may ask for any correction to what she has said thus far and then may say something like this:

> Tell me what brings you here, the main things that may be troubling you, and how that is affecting you how you are feeling. I'll be listening carefully to what you say, but I may need to interrupt you with some questions along the way in order to understand what you're feeling.

The Use of Questions: Good and Bad Ways

Many pastors who have learned something about counseling along the way may have heard that questions are to be avoided in order to emphasize the importance and value of listening. It is more important to learn that there are good and bad questions. Questions are bad, in the sense of getting in the way of "care-full" listening, when they essentially are space fillers. This happens, for example, when the pastor gets impatient or uncomfortable with silence and compulsively has to fill the space. Questions are also bad or not useful when they appear to be factual or objective information that is not a part of what the help seeker is telling about the problem or about himself. Curiosity not only kills the cat, it can kill the personal and relational character of a pastoral conversation. It's easy for most of us to get interested in the facts of the case and lose track of the person with whom we are developing a relationship. There is a more to be said about this because it is a very common problem, but that can be deferred until the discussion of later conversations.

Good questions are those that contribute to strengthening understanding more about the relationship. You should ask a question when you don't understand something the counselee has told you and you need to ask in order to understand what you are being told. This kind of question is one that can be "care-full" because it can convey that you really do want to understand not just what the person is saying but also the person himself. Sometimes the question is prefaced by an acknowledgment like, "I didn't understand what you meant when you said [whatever it was that you didn't understand]." That is a way of conveying that understanding the person and the problem requires all the involved persons working on it. Another good question is one that asks if the person telling about himself or his situation can slow down a bit. That also shows interest, but in addition it conveys the idea that this situation doesn't have to be worked on as an emergency. Something probably can be done but usually after thinking about it in a deliberative fashion.

Magic Questions: What Are You Looking for? Why Now? Why Me?

To get at what the help seeker is looking for in coming for counseling, the pastor should make use of some form of what I have called the "magic questions": What are you looking for? Why now? Why me? I don't remember where I first read or heard about these questions and began to make use of them. I do know that they are used in some form in most of the mental health disciplines for evaluating a patient and that they can be helpful to pastors as well. The questions certainly don't need to be asked in this form, but the pastor who does not make use of them in some way can get lost in trying to aid the person seeking help. The function of the "What are you looking for?" question is to allow both parties in the counseling relationship to realize that they don't have to deal with everything in a person's life—at least not now—but can focus on something in particular. That question is also an attempt to get to a serious answer for the usually social and casual question, "How are you?" by asking more specifically "How are you now?" "How are you experiencing pain or loss, and how is it affecting you?" The focus of the question is upon the present situation.

The pastor will be asking other questions as a part of her "care-full" listening. The purpose of such questioning is to develop a balance between allowing the person seeking help to express his concerns in his own way and structuring the conversation so that the pastor can understand it in her way. The questioning is usually less about gathering more information than it is about facilitating dialogue rather than monologue. There is some value in simply ventilating the problem, but developing a trusting, supportive relationship is more important. Without that effort toward dialogue it is too easy for the pastor to listen to a long recital of the person's concerns without having quite understood them and then be expected to answer the question, "What should I do now?". What the pastor is attempting is to have the participants talking about and clarifying the problem together.

Just as the function of the first question is to deal with the present, with what's happening now, the function of the second question, "Why now?" is to deal with the past. There was some time in the past when whatever is painful now was not going on. Something apparently happened to change things. This is often referred to as the "precipitating cause" of the problem. The pastoral questioner is attempting to guide the conversation into their thinking together about then and now and indirectly suggest that if things can be different in a negative direction, they can probably change in a positive direction as well.

As the reader might already be thinking, these guiding questions are often not immediately answered. Sometimes, in order to avoid the pain of the present, a person needs to begin with the past, or starting with the past may just be his style. "Let me tell you how all of this started." The pastor can afford to do that but not to lose track of the first question about how the person is now and what he wants. It's too easy to get lost in a person's history and, in the process, indirectly take on responsibility for remembering and dealing with all of it. Somewhere in hearing the "how it all started story" the pastor needs to say something like this:

> I understand most of what you're saying about how things used to be and what went wrong, but I need to be able to think with you about what's happening to you now and the pain you're feeling with that. Take a minute, and go back to how you're feeling now in the best way you can.

Sometimes this kind of interruption and redirection needs to happen several times. It's not an attempt to fill in the answers on a questionnaire. It's simply being sure that some understanding and answers to the questions don't get lost and that the participants in the conversation are moving toward dialogue about the present situation. People are interesting to most pastors, and it's easy to get interested in the details of what has happened in their history and what they have managed to accomplish in their life as a way of not dealing with their present pain. Most important, as the pastor has experienced in pastoral care, is to be present with the person, with his problem or pain, particularly at the beginning of the counseling. If that takes place, a trusting dialogue about whatever needs to be discussed can go on.

Another thing involved in trying to stay with the sequence of present first and then deal with the past is that it is a useful way to determine the seriousness of the present problem. The pastor does not need to think in psychological diagnostic terms. What she should try to determine is how well this person is functioning in life right now. How much anxiety does he have? What's the level of his sadness about life or depression? How accurate do his perceptions about life seem? What, if any, kind of feelings is his situation stirring in the pastor? Does hearing the counselee's pain make her feel anxious or hopeless about the situation? These are the kind of things that the pastor should be in touch with in a first meeting with a person. Some other things related to these kinds of evaluative questions will be dealt with in the chapters on possible follow-up sessions. In this first session, however, the pastor is already beginning to think about whether or not she is the one to continue with this situation or if this is one that will need a referral to a more experienced, professional therapist.

Who Is the Most Appropriate Helper for This Person?

The thought about referral or "Who is the most appropriate helper for this person?" leads naturally into the third "magic question": "Why me?" So the pastor asks, at some time during the first meeting, "How did you happen to decide to come and talk to me?" On some occasions the person seeking help will give the reason for choosing to come to see the pastor without having been asked. Most of the time, however, the pastor will need to take the initiative and ask. In discussing pastoral counseling with many students and pastors, I have found that a majority of them are uncomfortable and hesitant to ask this question. That seems to be because somewhere in their lives they were taught that it's not good manners to pay too much attention to yourself. What the pastor is doing, however, is paying attention to the relationship, and with this question demonstrating, without having to say too much: "The relationship between us and what I represent is more important than my being able to answer your question or solve the problem that you have presented."

Asking this very practical question about how the counselee happened to choose her to talk to is also a way that the pastor communicates that paying attention to relationships is important and is one of the main things they will be doing in the counseling, namely, noticing things about relationships and talking about them honestly. One of the things that is a part of many or most problems is that so many people have very little experience in talking about the relationships that are most important to them. The pastor's developing relational wisdom requires her to constantly look for ways to talk honestly about relationships and find ways to encourage those with whom she counsels to do the same.

The "Why me?" question, and being able to discuss it, contributes to putting trust in the pastor should she need to refer the person seeking help to a helper, one who may have more training and experience in dealing with a particular type of problem. This question of "here or elsewhere" should be begun in the first counseling session, but it may need to be a part of all of the sessions that the pastor conducts. It is clear that before the first session is completed the pastor needs to convey the idea that she may indeed need to refer.

What is going on in this more structured way of listening to a person through the use of the questions—What are you looking for? Why now? Why me?—is further acquaintance with the problem and the person. It is like what in mental health counseling would be called the diagnostic process, but for pastors in their context for ministry it should not be done in mental health terminology. The pastor is attempting through evaluation to construct a road map that may be used by both parties in the counseling for what may be ahead of them in the counseling and also in the seeker's life situation.

The initial pastoral counseling conversation is a way of beginning this process. Pastoral counselors attempt to hear and demonstrate their understanding of the way a person has constructed his world, give an alternate understanding that is enough like the counselee's way of putting things together so that it can be accepted as being accurate, and gently give back to the counselee the ongoing task of reconstructing his world and living in it. It may be thought of as a revisioning of the counselee's story and putting it into a more intelligent, more imaginative plot. That can, in effect, create a more interesting and challenging world in which to live. Pastoral counseling at its best can move from an essentially passive way of thinking about a person's life to a more active one in which he can be viewed as a mover and changer of things.

If counseling is pursued beyond the initial meeting, what has been discussed in evaluating the situation contributes to the development of a common language for talking about the person's life so that the participants understand each other better. If counseling terminates after a first meeting, the road map constructed may be used by the counselee for living life itself without a counseling relationship. In either case, the process of putting together a new picture of one's life situation that is continuous with old views but leads beyond them may have significant value.

Evaluation as a Part of the Structure

Evaluation in pastoral counseling is not a process of naming a problem or some objective identification of a person as this or that. Rather, it may be thought of as a dialogical task of both counselor and counselee as they attempt to develop a common language about the counselee's life situation. It is not a judgment arrived at by the pastor in order to determine what treatment to apply in the case. Simply stated, it is the pastor and the person seeking help while trying to talk more effectively together about what's going on and what to do about it.

Evaluation focuses on the problem that is presented, but it also contributes to not losing touch with the larger issues in the life of the person in the process of attending to the counselee's immediate concern. Pastoral counseling involves maintaining an awareness of the picture a person paints of himself and finding appropriate ways to share that awareness together. The pastor has a special interest in and commitment to religious concerns, but her ongoing evaluative concern is to formulate ways to allow persons to see and talk about themselves in relation both to religious and also to other convictions about life.

Using an evaluative structure in pastoral counseling can contribute in three ways to the counseling itself and often to changing a person's life situation:

1. It facilitates the building of relationship through the sharing of a person's story, feelings, and hopes.

2. It contributes to a person's seeing the problem he has presented as a part of his larger life story and as both internal and external to himself.

3. It can aid in the discovery and acceptance of what is common and what is unique in his life situation, thus contributing to understanding what can and what cannot be changed.

Evaluative Structure as Contributor to Relationship

An evaluative structure for the counseling meeting can contribute to developing the relationship between the pastor and the person seeking help by offering some control over the way the counselee's vulnerability is revealed. Many pastors and most hospital chaplains have had the experience of a patient in a hospital or in some other crisis situation expressing his problem and feelings in an uncontrolled kind of way. In some ways it was good that he could "get it out," but in other ways it was probably too much too soon. On a visit soon after that the same person often acts as if he hardly knows that pastor or chaplain. That's because in some ways he hardly does know her, and their relationship needs to be developed more slowly. What can and should happen in pastoral counseling is that the pastor structures the situation so that problem and person are revealed in a more controlled, less threatening way. A pastor who works at doing that creates confidence in the other person that things are not going to get out of hand and that, at least in terms of relationships, the pastor knows what she is doing.

Expressing Feelings, Not Just Talking about Others

Another part of the pastor's attempt to think about seeker's problem in the context of his whole life situation is trying to focus upon what the person himself feels rather than talking primarily about others. Another way to think about this is by contrasting what the pastor is trying to do in her counseling with what a police officer or lawyer is trying to do: namely, to get the facts. The pastor is not uninterested in the facts of the problem situation, but she is more concerned with getting the feelings that the counselee is having about the situation. Many people are uncomfortable in expressing their feelings and try to avoid doing so by attempting to be objective and more detached from what they are describing. In keeping with the experience she already has in doing pastoral care with persons in a crisis situation, the pastor's focus should be upon the affective rather than the objective. This is a concern that should be a part of all of the counseling, however long it takes place.

A simple but extremely helpful thing to notice in a first counseling conversation is how a problem is presented. Is it located externally or internally? "My problem is out there" and "my problem is all me" are extreme ways of defining one's human situation, which can mark two ends of an evaluative continuum. The pastor can find it useful to make some judgment as to where on the continuum of external or internal problem definition the counselee is located. One of her primary goals in pastoral counseling is to assist the person consulting her in redefining the problem as realistically as possible so that, following Reinhold Niebuhr's familiar words, he may change the things that can be changed, accept the things that cannot be changed, and have the wisdom to know one from the other.

Probably the most common presentation is an external location of the problem. Virtually every pastor can recall a conversation in which the person consulting her said something like, "My problem is my husband." In the initial statement of what is wrong there is little or nothing said about the person presenting the problem. Everything is external to her. This kind of presentation is not limited to family problems. For parish ministers it may happen most often with problems about what's happening in the church where she serves. Someone to whom the presenter is related is not doing her job properly, or it may be a whole group of "someones" who are presented as at fault. It is likely that most persons who consult their pastor are realistic enough not to locate the problem somewhere apart from themselves without acknowledging some participation in it themselves. Initially, however, their participation is presented as a limited involvement. The person seems to be saying, "Certainly I have some responsibility for what has happened, but not much. Most of the problem is out there or at least in the part of me that is not my real self."

One of the most important things for pastors to think about in evaluating how a problem or situation is presented is noticing whether the person is able to express what he has observed or felt or is simply describing something "they" have done. With the woman whose first presentation of the problem located it externally to her husband, the pastor might say, "Can you tell me how the way your husband is affects you? What are you feeling when that's going on?" Early into the discussion of the problem, the pastor attempts to get the person seeking help to talk about herself. If she can succeed in this or even move in this direction, the pastor will be contributing to the counselee's ability to get something useful from the counseling relationship. The pastor's question or intervention into the description of the problem is usually not successful on the first or second attempt, but it is something that the pastor needs to come back to. It will be discussed again in the next chapter, which will discuss more about hearing and responding to the particular ways problems are presented.

At this point we are simply looking at the question of external or internal location of the problem and the pastor's beginning to think about how she may be able to help this person think about and experience the problem in a more balanced way. The more the counselee can talk about how he is experiencing and feeling in relation to the problem the more likely he and the pastor can make it a part of their relationship and work on it together. When the counselee can express his own pain, it is more likely that the pastor can be present with his pain just as he might do in a pastoral-care hospital visit.

Less frequently encountered are the persons who see themselves, usually quite unrealistically, as responsible for everything that is going on. They seem to be saying that their inadequacy is so great that virtually every unfortunate thing that has happened to their families or on their job is really their fault. They avoid analysis of the problem and, in effect, the possibility of change, by simplistically laying all blame on themselves. If they are so inadequate as persons, they couldn't possibly do anything about changing things, and they imply that certainly the pastor will need to do something about that.

The temptation for the pastor with a person who is locating the problem within herself is to be overcome with the confession of inadequacy and try in some way to argue with it—to quickly try countering what the person says she is feeling. This is generally quite ineffective. In the next chapter we will be dealing with a more effective way of dealing with this through learning about the person and looking for strengths that might be used in dealing with what's going on. At this point when the pastor is evaluating the person and problem, she is simply thinking about a way of coming at things later should the person feel enough support in the counseling to want to some back for other pastoral conversations.

The pastor needs to be on the lookout for physical or emotional abuse, particularly in a person who seems to put too much of the problem on herself. It is very common for such persons to try to hold on to an abusive relationship through self-blame and by excusing the other, often the marital partner. This may be explored in more detail in any later meetings, but in an initial conversation, the pastor needs to ask more about it and begin to present the idea of a referral to a person or agency that regularly deals with abuse.

What Is Common and What Is Unique about This Person?

Although evaluation in pastoral counseling is not labeling or classifying, there are inevitably ways in which thinking about one person's life or problem or situation as like others can be helpful. When counselees come to a helping person of any type, they hope, sometimes desperately, that their problem will sound familiar.

Having a structure for what happens in a meeting for counseling is usually quite helpful in assisting the person seeking help to realize and accept that he is not the only one who has this problem. This usually happens when he senses from the pastor's manner, more than from her words, that she is comfortable in talking about persons' feelings because she has done that many times before. When a person seeking help is asked in a second meeting with a pastor what he remembers about their first meeting, frequently the person will express his satisfaction that the pastor seemed familiar with the kind of problem he described. However, less frequently heard is the complaint that the pastor seemed a bit too familiar with the problem. Probably, it is heard less frequently because many of these people did not come back for a second meeting, perhaps because they did not feel that the pastor was sufficiently respectful of the uniqueness of their pain and too quickly responded as if their pain was like everybody else's. This alternative interpretation is clearly something that the pastor needs to keep in mind.

The fact that other persons have similar problems can be supportive as long as the sense of "my particular problem is special" is not lost. A wise psychotherapist once observed, "Everybody wants to be special." Virtually everyone seeking help feels in some way or another, "I am the only one to whom this has happened, and I need special attention." That need to be special may be recognized within the context of the pastor's manner conveying that she has been there before, but it should be done without the pastor's talking about other persons' problems or her own.

The pastoral counselor's task is to respect the need to be special and to try to understand the particular expressions of that need when it is encountered. The burden of the pastoral relationship, the evaluative process, and the process of counseling itself are to help this person or persons to discover, without losing the sense of their unique value, that other persons share that problem.

Probably the most important questions in assessing a person who has come for counseling are: "How well is this person functioning, both as she thinks of herself and as others observe and think of her?" "How is she like or different from others with whom she is likely to be comparing her life situation?" And then, "What's going on in relation to this level of function?" "How much is the lostness she is experiencing getting in the way of her living her life as well as she wants to live it?" If there is sadness or depression evident, it is important to get some description of what that is like, particularly keeping in mind those questions about function. With respect to a couple, "How are they alike or different from each other, and how do these differences help or hurt their relationship?" Most of these questions won't need to be asked directly but will be answered as the person tells his story. "Is there a pattern of abuse of self or others? How much anxiety or worry is the person experiencing?" Describing the problem, the feelings associated with it, and its effects on person and family are all important to being helpful.

What Language to Use in Thinking about This Person and Problem

Another useful question for the pastor while doing counseling has to do with what kind of language to use. Since pastoral counseling may occur because of who the pastor is and the religious community she represents, the language and concepts out of a particular religious tradition may be helpful in clarifying the understanding of a person's problem and personal style. The language of one of the historic prayers of the church, for example, may be useful in that it describes in a practical way a person's style of life. The prayer says that "we have not done the things that we ought to have done, we have done the things that we ought not to have done, and there is no health in us." Some of the persons that the pastor counsels with are more "not done" people and others are "have done" people. The prayer's words about there being "no health in us" is not saying that there is nothing good in either type of person but that the brokenness is not located in just one place. It extends to the whole person and has both theological and psychological relevance.

The problem with using such language in dialogue with a person seeking help is that its meaning is sophisticated and sometimes obscure—satisfying to those who understand it but something that can get in the way of the counseling dialogue for those who do not. In this case, the dialogue will be more successful if it takes place in the language of ordinary life. Another possibility is that the use of religious language will be introduced by persons for whom being a part of a religious community is a significant aspect of their life, and they think that they need to talk with a pastor about what's happening to them in religious terms. Unfortunately, their use of religious language can often obscure understanding of what is actually bothering them.

Another thing the counseling pastor will note in most evaluative sessions is that there is not just one problem. Although it is important to keep in mind what answer the pastor heard for the "What are you looking for?" question, there will seldom be just one problem to talk about. And that's good news, not bad. It means that the person seeking help is beginning to trust the pastor with more of his life, not just his problem but also his hopes and dreams. This enables the pastor to do more of what was probably a part of her call to ministry, not being a problem solver but one who uses her relational wisdom to talk with persons about how they live their lives. Talking seriously about one problem usually makes a person think about other concerns and realize that he is not just discussing a problem but talking about himself.

As I suggested earlier, pastoral counseling can be thought of as, in some way, similar to the biblical book of Proverbs. Both are based on a faith in God and a sense of God's presence in life, but their language is not primarily religious. It is the practical language of ordinary life, a language easy to understand. Certainly there is some trickiness and cleverness in Proverbs that can be helpful in a public discourse and yet get in the way of common understanding in the more private context of counseling. Nevertheless, both are intended to offer relational wisdom in life's more common language. Specialized language, such as in medicine, religion, psychology, and other technical fields can sometimes give a more nearly accurate and objective picture of a person's life situation, but ordinary language shared by both parties can be more understandable and satisfying.

Sometimes in simple, everyday language there are symbols used that point to deeper meanings, and both in pastoral care and counseling the pastor needs to be on the lookout for that kind of language and its meaning to the person who uses it. Chaplains in an institutional setting have often heard the request from patients who had little or no experience talking about prayer that they be remembered. Those patients seemed to be asking for some kind of religious intervention but while avoiding the use of religious terminology.

An example of using nonreligious terminology to talk about one's life comes from a visit with an elderly farmer who, in telling the pastor about his life, said that when he was growing up his family was so poor that they couldn't have biscuits for breakfast. They had to eat cornbread. The pastor understood that nearing the end of his life he was celebrating how far he had been able to come in spite of a hard beginning. He had grown up with cornbread, but now his life was full of biscuits made with white flour.

41

The pastor's relational wisdom involves recognizing that a person can talk seriously about life and it's meaning without talking explicitly about relationship with God.

What to Do at the End of the First Meeting

Having said at the beginning of the meeting how much time she had available that day, about ten to fifteen minutes before the ending time, the pastor should say something like this: "It is about the time that I need to end our meeting together. I want to go over some of things I have heard as we have discussed what's troubling you. Let me know if I have understood you correctly, and then we need to think together about the possibility of our meeting again to work on this problem." Following through on what she has said about the time available for the session indicates that the pastor is comfortably in control of the way that the counseling is being conducted and with what is being discussed. The purpose of this kind of statement is certainly to find out whether or not the pastor has understood the problem correctly, but perhaps more important, to experience the value of pastor and counselee having a satisfying working relationship in thinking about the counselee's life.

The pastor then gives a review of what has been discussed together, the way the person has described the problem and, insofar as possible, the counselee's feelings about the situation. The pastor asks about the accuracy of what she has said and if there is anything that the counselee would add to what has been said and, if necessary, dialogue about that. Then, if the pastor feels comfortable in further dealing with the situation as presented thus far, she asks about whether or not the counselee would like to come in for another meeting about this.

If the pastor is asked whether or not she thinks they should continue to meet, it is usually important to encourage the counselee to make that choice. If she is asked for her opinion on the matter, something simple like, "I think it could be useful" might be said. Or if the pastor believes that it would be better for a more experienced helping professional to deal with the situation from this point on, she should say this and suggest a particular person that she knows or knows about and how to reach that person.

Finally, if she can do this honestly, not just as a formality, the pastor should express her appreciation to the person for sharing something of his life with her in this difficult time. And again, if this is true for her, say that she customarily prays for people who are living through a difficult situation and that she will pray for this person at her regular prayer time or now if he wishes. If she prays there, it is important to be simple and direct, not distancing herself by a prayer that could seem like the application of what ministers usually say but briefly relating the prayer to the concerns of the meeting.

Chapter Three

Continuing the
Counseling Conversation

Although the major concern of this chapter is how to proceed with pastoral counseling that continues beyond the first meeting, the chapter will continue to remind the pastor that in counseling he is not doing something new. He is doing something he is familiar with—pastoral care—but doing it in a different way, with a more clearly defined structure. In both care and counseling the pastor is responding to a person's lostness—in some way having been separated from community, significant relationships, a sense of meaning and purpose in life. The difference between care and counseling is that in counseling a person has asked for help, and the pastor responds to the problem by developing a structure for the counseling conversation.

Beginning a Second Meeting
for Counseling

Recall that in the last few minutes of their first conversation, the pastor modeled what he wants to encourage in the counselee by telling her what he has heard from her in their meeting. He then asked the counselee to think about what she had heard from him and to correct anything that did not seem to express what she had been experiencing or feeling. The pastor didn't say, "If you are going to get help from an interpersonal process like counseling you have to reflect on your experience and talk about it with me." He simply tried to model some reflection of their experience together and encouraged the counselee to do the same.

Similarly, in the first few minutes of a second pastoral counseling session, the pastor attempts to build on what was done before and, after any initial social response that began their meeting, asks the counselee to share with him any thoughts she has had about their first meeting or anything that seemed to have resulted from it. There are a variety of questions or comments that can be made that are related to this, for example, "What do you remember about our last meeting together?" "Is there anything that you said or I said that stuck with you after the meeting?" "Did anything happen between the last time we met and now that seems to be related to our getting together?" Any questions of the kind that can encourage remembering and connecting what happened then to what's happening now can be useful.

This way of beginning is similar to what may be said at the beginning of a scheduled group meeting, in a church or elsewhere: "Are there any additions or corrections to the minutes?" It is a procedural way of connecting one meeting with another and conveying the idea that what happens in one meeting should connect with what happened in a previous one. Although there is a similarity in what happens in an official group meeting to what happens in pastoral counseling, an important difference in what happens in the latter is that no records of the content of the meeting should be kept. The only appropriate records for a pastor to keep are the time and place of meeting and the names and relationship of other family members.

The No Records Recommendation

The reason for this "no records recommendation" is, on one hand, because of the expectation of secrecy and confidentiality in the relationship between a pastor and a parishioner that is in some way a part of the tradition of the confessional. In addition to that, a pastor's or a chaplain's office does not usually have the same kind of standards for confidentiality that a mental health clinic or counseling center does. Records may be needed in a mental health or counseling center setting, but written records objectify the person seeking help by allegedly giving objective or factual information about her and her problem. In pastoral counseling, when it is understood as a part of pastoral care, the focus is not so much on how the counseling and her problem are described, but upon the relationship between pastor and counselee and other relationships that are discussed in the meeting. This means that the pastor who does counseling in his usual setting for ministry needs to work on facilitating his memory. The ability of the counselee and pastor to reflect and remember together is a positive indicator that pastoral counseling may have a valuable outcome.

After the questions and responses regarding what the participants remember about the last session, the pastor listens to anything the counselee has to say about what is happening now. The counselee may have a lot or very little to say. In both of those cases the pastor needs to keep in mind the answers given to the "magic questions" of the first session. He will probably not ask them again in the same way he did the first time, but it is important to keep them in mind. He might say something like, "The last time we met you said a great deal about the pain you were experiencing in the relationship with your daughter. Does that relationship seem about the same, or are there some differences?" This question shows that the pastor was paying attention to what was said before and is assuming that some changes in the way a relationship is experienced can happen. Discussion of the question further assumes that although no "what to do about it" responses to the problem have yet been proposed, just having some company to share feelings with and to think together about the problem is usually helpful.

Sometimes in response to the "how are things going now?" question the person changes the focus of her concern, realizing that what she first presented is just one part of a theme of painful relationships with persons in the family or coming up with something else that at first seems completely unrelated. Again the pastor involves all of his listening skills, trying to respond to the new facet of the problem in a way that focuses more upon the feelings about it than the facts of the case. In the listening process, although he probably doesn't say anything about this the first time he is aware of it, he is searching for any apparent strengths in the person describing the problem. This is something he will want to emphasize later as they are discussing what can be done about the problem.

Structuring the Conversation for Effective Listening

If the person has had a lot to say about what she remembers and where the situation seems to be now, the pastor may need to employ some more questions in order to structure the situation in a way that he can better understand it. Again this is similar to what should also happen in the listening that goes on in pastoral care. For most pastors, if they simply listen passively to long stories or descriptions, it is very easy to get lost in the details and lose track of what the person's central concern is. Some of this has been said earlier in the book, but in pastoral counseling, dialogue is almost always better than monologue, and what the pastor is attempting to facilitate is a relationship where two persons are talking and thinking together about a life situation. In order to do this the pastor often needs to break into the counselee's monologue and ask questions about particular parts of it so that he can be connected with what is being described.

If the person has little or no response to the question of what is happening now or "What do you remember about our time together?" the pastor will have to work harder than with the person who talks more easily. The work will be focused on the question the pastor must have in mind but probably will not say anything about at this point: "How can we develop a way of thinking about this problem together?" It's usually not very useful to try to get with why this person doesn't remember or won't say what she remembers about the counseling time together and what it stirred up in her life. More often than not it reflects the difficulty the counselee has in asking for and using support through relationships. How the pastor responds to this will have a lot to do with his own particular style in getting to know people.

Getting the Story

It may be useful to think of this section of the conversation as "getting the person's story." How has the person lived her life, and what are some of the significant features of it? Obviously, this getting the story is not unique to the counseling experience. It is a part of everyday pastoral work. In counseling, it is the same thing, only more so. The pastor has to be interested in what's wrong because that is the ostensible reason a person has consulted him. His interest, however, is both broader and deeper. It lies in how this person is trying to live her life in relation to particular persons and to God. A significant part of the pastor's calling to ministry is thinking of persons' lives in that way, but it is not necessary to insist that the person he is trying to help think of it in that way or at this time. At this point in the counseling, a theological way of thinking about the situation is more a guide for the pastor than for the counselee.

One way of beginning to learn a person's story might be something like what some of the writers about family therapy have called "joining," or simply trying to connect with persons in a family by finding some common interests or experiences. The pastor might say, "I'd like to think with you about how you can deal with the problem you presented, but it would help me understand better if you could tell me more about the rest of your life." The pastor is trying to find a way to put the presented problem in context. How is it like anything that has happened before? What strengths or weaknesses did the person show in dealing with previous problems? As a part of this filling out the context of the problem, the pastor will then try to get something more of the person's history and notice what has been important to her in life. What has she tried to achieve, and how successful does she feel that she has been? What has helped her or hurt her in that process of living life and in identifying and achieving her goals? This is certainly some of what the pastor will do with persons who more freely express themselves and who seem to remember and connect events in their lives, but with the less verbally expressive person he will have to be more persistent.

More about "Care-Full" Listening

The previous chapter used the term and briefly touched on the meaning of "care-full" listening. Although this kind of listening should have been a part of the counseling conversation from its beginning, in a second meeting, when some sense of structure for the counseling been established, more needs to be said about it. Care involves both careful attention to the person cared for and the pastor's awareness of himself and what he is feeling during the conversation. That involves awareness he has of his own anxiety about the issue he is being consulted about and what he may be conveying to another about who and what he is as a person.

In this further discussion of "care-full" listening it is important to note again the value of trying to take seriously a question that is usually taken only casually and encouraging the other person to respond seriously to "How *are* you?" The pastor is asking himself, "How easily can this person talk seriously about that with me?" The particular concern here, without losing touch with the problem that brought the person to counseling, is to listen for the larger issues of life and faith—the person's anxiety about life, the "to be or not to be" or "how to be" questions. The pastor in this kind of listening is trying to convey that this person's whole being in relationship matters to him.

This type of listening is similar to some eyeglasses in that it is bifocal. It attends to the immediate situation but also listens for opportunities to consider larger issues, the longer vision in the counselee's life. The pastor is not called to care for persons by solving their problems. He is called to recognize and communicate by the way he listens—even in the most difficult circumstances—to what a person really is, a child of God created in and for relationship.

There is another way that listening should be bifocal. My way of putting it in conversations with pastors has been, "Pay attention to what happens after the 'but.'" To the seriously put "how are you?" question the counselee often answers, "I'm doing pretty well, I guess." And then there is a pause, or sometimes rather quickly comes a "but"—and a qualifying clause that begins to get to the counselee's pain or disappointment. The pastor has a choice to listen to the good news or the bad news, but "carefullness" usually means listening and responding to the bad news first.

This is in some ways similar to the way that Old Testament scholar Walter Brueggemann has pointed out that the Bible speaks about God and about the human situation in more than one way. There is a majority message and a different voice from the minority as well. As Bruegemann puts it, in the Bible there is both testimony and counter testimony—a voice of faith and a voice that challenges that faith, such as in the challenging, questioning voice of Job and in the skeptical, often cynical voice of the writer of Ecclesiastes. In the Psalms there are strong expressions of both—words of faith and those of anger, pain, and doubt (*Theology of the Old Testament: Testimony, Dispute, Advocacy* [Minneapolis, MN: Augsburg/Fortress, 1997]). The voices in the New Testament are more unified in their testimony to Jesus as the Christ, but even here there is sometimes a minority voice of questioning and doubt. It may be heard in the doubt of the disciple Thomas or sometimes even in the voice of the apostle Paul when in practical matters of the community of faith this man of faith seems a bit uncertain.

In his counseling conversations, the pastor should listen for both the majority and minority voices from the person seeking help. Much of his skill lies in hearing and responding not only to the testimonies of faith and the church but also the negative testimonies of grief, illness, and broken relationships. Effective listening requires being present with both the positive and negative. Although what the pastor represents is the language of faith and the church, in the ministry of pastoral care he is called to listen even more carefully to the counter testimony to faith: the negative, uncertain, and doubtful voice.

In the sixth chapter of the book of Job, Job rejects the quick answers to his problems that are proposed by his friends. He accuses them of betraying him and says plainly in Job 6:21: "You see something awful and are afraid" (CEB). Most of those to whom we listen do not speak as clearly and assertively as did Job, but his words are a valuable reminder that the situation of many of those for whom we are to care stirs our anxiety and reminds us of our own vulnerability. One of the challenges of effective caring is to listen for and hear the counter testimony to faith in persons' lives as well as their testimony. This is what the pastor needs to do in both care and counseling.

The ability of the pastor to listen and respond to a person's bad news contributes to his being able to look for the good. Response to the bad is most often a response to the counselee's feelings, feelings of lostness or hopelessness or failure to find any positive direction in her situation. Response to the good comes later when the pastor has heard something that the counselee has done that seems to have made the situation better. It is seldom helpful to speak generally and say something like "I'm sure it's going to get better" when the reason for saying that grow more out of the pastor's own need to feel better. That is ineffective and empty reassurance to give because it grows out of the counselor's feelings of inadequacy and needing to do something.

Good and effective reassurance comes when the pastor has observed or heard from the counselee about something she had done to address the problem. Doing something, whatever it may have been, made her feel better and eventually might contribute to solving the problem. For example, take the situation of a person in midlife who had lost a job that had been very satisfying to her and has come to the pastor with a great deal of discouragement and depression. On a second meeting for counseling, after the pastor's asking about what has happened in the time since their first meeting, the counselee says that she has come up with a plan for contacting a wide variety of acquaintances who might be able to suggest a direction she could go in looking for a job. The counselee might or might not say that doing something made her feel better, but in hearing about what has been done the pastor is able to offer reassurance based on her actual behavior. If he feels it and can honestly say it, the pastor may say, "I'm impressed that you're not just sitting but are moving. We don't know what results you will have yet, but thoughtful action is almost always good."

The pastor then can use his own judgment about waiting for more from the counselee or going on and continuing to emphasize the importance of action and connection with other persons. "There are a couple of other things that you might consider doing. Plan your day so that there are two or three things that you schedule yourself to do and then carry them out. They won't all have to do with the job search, but they should be things that can make your life better. One of them is a regular plan for exercise, particularly walking or running. It is important that you try to avoid just sitting still and letting things happen. Action is one of the best correctives for sadness or depression."

Pastoral Assessment of Function

Although the assessment of a person's mental health in psychological terms is not a necessary part of the pastor's counseling ministry, some practical assessment of a person's ability to carry out the usual functions of her life should be a natural part of what he does. Other than the various limits that may be imposed by physical health, the most common limits to everyday function are anxiety and depression. Therefore, at this point in the counseling conversation it is important to attempt to make some judgment about them. Does the person seem more anxious or depressed, and to what degree do anxiety and/or depression interfere with doing the things the counselee needs to do in everyday life?

A practical way of doing this is to begin by asking something like, "How is the problem you're experiencing affecting your ordinary life, things like eating and sleeping, following your usual routine of keeping the necessities of life going, being with people, and getting some satisfaction out of relationships?" The pastor's experience in crisis pastoral care in illness and grief will help him in this talk about behavior that is seemingly not related to the problem as it was first presented. It is similar to the kinds of things people talk about in visits with the sick and grieving. If some impairment in basic functioning is reported, the pastor should ask what, if anything, the counselee has tried to do to make things better. If she is doing something to improve her function, referral to another helper may not be needed. If she is not taking at least some action to improve things herself, the pastor should go farther in questioning her so that she can become more aware of the way that she functions in life. This can also pave the way for a referral to a professional mental health counselor who has more time to further this process of self-reflection.

Observing Behavior

Something the pastor and counselee will probably not talk about, although it should be noticed, is the counselee's appearance. If the pastor knows the person from acquaintance in the church or some other place, he should think about the question, "Does she look like herself?" Is there any significant difference in appearance between now and other times they may have met? If the way a person looks seems to be deteriorating, this obviously suggests that need for help beyond what the pastor can give is indicated. Again, the pastor's experience in crisis pastoral care in illness and grief can help him in this. He should keep in mind that the key issue in assessing the need for further help is the person's ability to function, not optimally, but well enough to keep going in many of her usual ways. And particularly if the person herself is worried about how she is functioning, then it is important to move on toward providing an appropriate referral.

Paying Attention to Ways of Thinking

What we have been discussing here and what the pastor should have been thinking about at least at this point in counseling conversations is how well the person seems to be able to function in terms of behavior. A second thing to pay attention to is the way a person appears to be thinking. A mental health professional often makes use of some kind of mental status examination. The pastor may not use the usual question-and-answer form of the exam but will be listening for what some of the questions on that exam are getting at. Although the pastor is definitely not an examiner, he should be a listener and observer of how a conversation is taking place. That is a part of "care-full" listening. You don't have to ask about time and date in order to be aware of how well a person is in touch with such things. How much does the person forget as she attempts to tell the story of her life and present situation? Failure to remember what happened between counseling conversations may not be an indicator of a problem mental status, but just listening to the way an event is described and clarified in the conversation can be used to assess this. It's not the pastor's business to ask questions about mental status, but it is his business to notice indicators of that when they appear in the conversation about other things and if the person seems to be bothered by difficulty in remembering. At that point the pastor may ask more about this, not so much to be gathering objective facts but as something that he and the counselee are sharing in the context of their relationship.

Relationships and Feelings

A third thing to notice in this informal, relational assessment of the counselee's mental health status is the way that she deals with feelings and the way she makes contact with other persons. In pastoral care the pastor already has some experience with helping persons express their feelings. This is more in the area of the pastor's usual function than is what we noted in the assessment of behavioral function or mental status. As the person tells about her problem and the larger story of her life, of which the problem is a part, what feelings seem to be present? Sadness, anger, anxiety, joy, fear, shame, pride, and so on? Is the person able to own these feelings and express them or does she move away from them and talk about what someone else has done to cause them? It is almost always easier for a person to describe what someone else has done than to express her own feelings about what has been going on. If the counselee is aware of her feelings and can express them in relationship with the pastor, she may be well on the way of using the counseling to feel better about her problem and her life. A significant dimension of the pastor's relational wisdom is in his perceiving and discovering the meaning of a person's relationships, how they have seemed to function and how they are functioning now.

Getting the Problem into the Room

As we noted in the previous chapter, the pastor should begin in his first meeting with persons both to question them about their feelings and to encourage them to express them. It is too easy for the majority of persons to avoid the anxiety involved in acknowledging their feelings when it is so much easier to talk about what's wrong with the person or persons who are troubling them. In a situation of a woman complaining about her husband's lack of attention to her, the pastor might say in the second counseling conversation, "You've told me some things about your husband that are troubling you. Can you say more how that affects you when it happens and how it affects you now?"

Although that kind of question seems almost too obvious or simple for the pastor to feel comfortable in asking it, he does need to ask it. If he can get the problem into the room, not outside somewhere with someone else but between pastor and counselee discussing the problem together, something can be done about it. It may not directly change the problem behavior or the husband or whoever the person is troubled about, but the counselee can feel empowered by being with someone who seems to understand. And in getting beyond her lostness—feeling alone and help-less—she may be able to move from passivity to some kind of action that helps her deal with her life. This may be in getting her husband to come in for a family conference with the pastor and hearing from the pastor to whom he would refer them for couples' therapy. It may be in making some decision about where she can go and what she can do in her life without having to involve the husband in it. It is important that the pastor remember that although he has been and can continue to be helpful as a pastor, he is not a marriage and family therapist. He may be most helpful with this problem by encouraging the couple to get help elsewhere. There will be more discussion of dealing with family problems in the next chapter.

A final thing needs to be said here on evaluating how a person expresses what she is feeling and the way she makes contact with others. The pastor can learn some very useful things about that by observing how the counselee is related to him in their counseling conversation. This is something that professional psychotherapists do as an important part of their practice. Does it seem to the pastor that the counselee is talking to him or just talking? Again, the terms *dialogue* and *monologue* are useful. Does it feel like the persons in the room are connecting as they think together about the life situation of one of them? The pastor may say something like, "I wonder how the way we are talking now is similar or different from the way you talk about your life with others." His observing, learning, and occasionally commenting on how their communication is going can often contribute to improving communication in relationships outside the counseling.

With the man who has genuine difficulty in talking about what he is feeling, the pastor may note that he expresses most everything in objective terms, as if he were looking at whatever he's describing at a distance. The pastor might comment on this and ask if the counselee noticed that and if it ever got in the way of what he was trying to do or say. There might be a subsequent interaction about when it seems safe to express his feelings and when it does not. This kind of discussion can be helpful when the pastor uses whatever relational wisdom he has available for the discussion.

The pastor might notice that another person moves away from a topic whenever it seemed to get uncomfortable. It's not the pastor's business to try to move in and change that. In this kind of short-term pastoral counseling he simply uses the observation to guide his dialogue with the person. He may or may not comment on it, but he may ask the counselee if she noticed the same thing too and, if so, did that get in the way of what she wanted to communicate? Another observation with a person might be that the counselee sometimes seems to try to reduce tension or conflict even before she really knows what it is about. This communication about communication is something that may or may not be discussed with the counselee, but the observation and learning from it is a significant contributor to the development of relational wisdom.

More on Getting the Story

Because pastoral counseling involves the pastor's hearing something of the larger story of a person's life, the pastor's question from the beginning of the counseling relationship needs to be, "How does this problem or concern fit into the overall life pattern?" If not much of the broader story of this person's life has come up in the conversation thus far, the pastor needs to ask about it. Beginning with what he already may know about the person's life the pastor asks, "Tell me some more about where you have been and what you are trying to accomplish in your life right now so I can understand how this problem gets in the way of that."

In mental health counseling this part of the conversation would be thought of as getting a history. In pastoral care and counseling it's more hearing and sharing in the story of a life. If the counselee wonders about this and seems to want only to talk about the problem, the pastor can simply say, "I really need your help in putting this problem in the context of your past life and your hopes for the future." Then in trying to "get the story" there are many different ways of going at it. Some of the things that the pastor will be looking for are places, persons, and events that have formed the story. Where did the person grow up? In one or many places? In what kind of family? Which members of the family is he still in significant relation with? What things were important to the family? To the person himself? What was he good at? What was difficult for him? The family's physical health and his own health? Schools and work? Events that seem to have influenced his life? Values and goals? The place of religion and faith? There may be other things in the story that the pastor will want to ask about or focus on. The point of this is to get a picture of a life and a person, not just a problem.

Getting something of the person's larger life story as well as his problem is an important part of the pastor's remembering and relating significantly to that person, but sometimes it is quite difficult to get to the story with much sense of feeling about it. Ernest Schachtel, one of the theorists who argued against Freud's theory that we repress certain memories because they are threatening to us, has said instead that the reason we forget is because we have not developed adequate ways to describe and reflect upon the events of our lives and share them with others.

"Adult memory," he said, "reflects life as a road with occasional signposts and milestones rather than as the landscape through which this road has led." The memories of the majority of people "come to resemble increasingly the stereotyped answers to a questionnaire, in which life consists of time and place of birth, religious denomination, residence, educational degrees, job, marriage, number and birthdates of children, income, sickness, and death" (Earnest G. Schachtel, "On Memory and Childhood Amnesia," *A Study of Interpersonal Relations*, ed. Patrick Mullahy [New York: Hermitage Press, 1949], 12). The pastor is not uninterested in those questionnaire items but needs to move beyond them into a richer, more meaningful story. The hearing and telling of stories of life and faith is a part of the tradition that the pastor represents and an essential way of recovery from a person's lostness.

Talking Specifically and Concretely

Consciously or unconsciously many persons hide from themselves and others through generalizations. A major pastoral task in pastoral counseling, then, is assisting them in talking concretely about themselves by finding some of the symbols, stories, and myths in their lives. A personal symbol is a specific object or action that reminds one of who he or she is. A personal myth is a tradition, image, or story, something like the biblical image, "My father was a starving Aramean" (Deut 26:5 CEB), which calls up a particular time in the early history of the Hebrew people and can give persons a sense of who they are and to what they belong. Such an image or symbol is a means of communicating who one is, who one is identified with, and how that person functions. These symbols may appear in the pastoral conversation in a number of ways, usually in something specific that the parishioner or counselee says about himself or herself, which a carefully attentive pastor should notice and be able to comment on then or later.

Equally important, however, is an active search for anything in what the person is sharing that captures the pastor's imagination and using that symbol or story in his mind as a new way of thinking about that person. This can enable the pastor to have an image of the person that transcends her problem. The problem is not ignored but is put in a perspective that sees it in relation to other dimensions of a person's life. While the unconscious dynamics of pastoral relationships are also important, the discovery of symbol, story, and myth does not negate but complements pastoral understanding. Stories and symbols give the pastor a way of seeing the dignity and humanity of a person in situations where dignity and humanity seem almost lost.

The second important thing about hearing and remembering a person's larger story involves hearing it, as we have suggested earlier, as a part of a dialogue rather than as a monologue. As we have suggested earlier, "care-full" listening usually involves interrupting and questioning about the story as well as listening to it. By questioning the counselee about particular parts of the story, the pastor is not primarily trying to "fill in all the blanks" in the person's history but to connect with particular parts of the story that interest her, in order to have better ways to remember the person and some of the issues in her life. There may be a person or place in the story that the pastor knows about. He can ask more about that in order to stay connected. The two persons involved in the conversation may share a common interest or value in nutrition, music, or whatever it is, and that may help the pastor remember and stay connected to the person. The pastor should look for things in the story to be interested in so that he can be in genuine dialogue about them and thus be more in touch with the person's life.

The Kinds of Lostness a Pastor May Be Consulted About

The most important purpose of this chapter is to remind the pastor that in both care and counseling he is responding to a person's lostness or separation from community, from significant relationships, from a sense of meaning and purpose in life. Whatever the problem that is presented as the reason for coming to counseling, the lostness experienced with the problem is something the pastor as pastor is familiar with. It's what religious ministry deals with whether in preaching, teaching, leading a faith community, or in counseling. So the pastor can think that with most any problem presented he is in some ways in familiar territory—addressing some expression of the general human condition.

Virtually all of the persons who consult the pastor for counseling are suffering from some type or degree of anxiety, depression, or both, and it is important to have some knowledge about them. The pastor needs to be thinking from the beginning of the counseling about whether or not the person needs more specialized treatment of the anxiety or depression that may be evident to him. His concern from the beginning of the counseling on to its conclusion is how well the person is functioning in spite of the problem and whether or not the support of and relationship to the pastor and the religious community he represents will be sufficient to improve the life situation. The pastor's task is to continue to offer pastoral care through the consultation he offers, including, when appropriate, connecting or referring the person seeking help to more specialized or problem-focused help.

In what follows I will not be presenting specific case studies of problems that the pastor may face. That can best be done in some kind of group consultation that allows for discovering how many different individual responses of group members can offer valuable consultation on how to think about and respond to a particular life situation. This book is simply calling attention to some of the general types of situations that pastors are confronted with and suggesting how whatever relational wisdom the pastor may offer can be useful. This kind of didactic consultation does not take the place of finding a consultant or consultant group that can offer face-to-face consultation on the pastor's particular life and ministry.

Using the Pastor's Acquaintance with Grief

As we have said in some way throughout the book, a pastor's overall calling to a parish or other place of ministry involves being in touch with the lives of members of that community. What he does in counseling is a part of the pastoral care that he offers to the whole community for and to which he is responsible and why we link pastoral counseling closely to the kind of care with which the pastor is familiar. Most frequently this is a problem that is in some way related to the loss of a significant person due to illness, disability, or death. The ministry is probably more acquainted with loss and grief than is any other profession. Consequently, the pastor is often the one to be approached for counseling related to grief by someone who has been told, "It's been long enough. You ought to be over it." The pastor needs to keep in mind that what he is doing in counseling is much the same as what he tried to do in pastoral care: encourage the expression of feelings, particularly after friends and family members feel that the person experiencing loss should be through with grieving.

The main difference between what the pastor does in this kind of counseling and in pastoral care is, again, that in counseling there needs to be more structure. Remembering and talking about the person lost goes on in counseling as it does in pastoral care, but it happens in a more matter-of-fact way. The feeling is there, but less intense or out of control, and there is usually more of an attempt to relate the loss to what the person is planning to do now. The pastor slowly attempts to expand the frame of how the person is thinking about her life. He avoids hurrying with this, but clearly has thinking and planning about the future as a part of what he does in the interaction. In contrast to dealing with other problems, he may structure further meetings with the person with longer intervals between them. The orientation becomes a consultation on life as it is emerging at different times after the time of the actual loss.

Another part of this consultation on life is dealing with anticipated loss as a result of a chronic physical and/or mental condition. The caregiver who consults with the pastor may be dealing with her fatigue as well as any depression or anxiety associated with the situation. The caregiver also may be dealing with mixed feelings about wishing it were all over and at the same time wanting to hold on to what's left in the caring relationship. There may also be mixed feelings among the family members about what to do now and some conflict related to any differences present. This is both familiar and unfamiliar territory in which the pastor can make use of all the relational wisdom he has available. There is quite probably no clear answer or direction to take, and the pastor's task, as in pastoral care, is to be calmly present in the ambiguity.

Another problem with loss that a pastor is quite often consulted about is the loss of a job or the loss of some kind of hope for a particularly meaningful career. Sometimes this may be related to retirement. Sometimes it may be related to a couple moving past childbearing age without having a child. There are a variety of important losses other than death, and they are all the kind of things that persons might talk about with a pastor who is able to use some wisdom about life and relationships to be present with persons. Most of what the pastor knows about and has experienced in ministry to those who are grieving can be employed in this counseling situation. The main difference is that the loss of a hope or dream may not seem to be as justifiable a reason for grief as the loss of a person. This is one reason that the pastor's availability to understand and talk about this kind of loss can be particularly important to the grieving person. The "blessing" of this kind of grief can often empower the person to go on to what is still possible for her now.

Problems at Work

The pastor may also be consulted about problems in a person's work situation. Two things are involved here. The first is being able to get genuinely interested in the problem that is presented and finding ways to understand it, not so much objectively but rather as something that is bothering this person in a particular way. As we have suggested earlier, developing this genuine interest requires careful discernment of the details of the problem and the ability to say to the counselee what you have understood.

Based on a common understanding of the problem, if it can be achieved, the second thing that the pastor can offer is dialogue about the problem that can break through the feeling of the counselee that she has to face it alone. Usually the work problem will have to do with relationships that the pastor has some general, if not specific, knowledge about. What is meant here about general knowledge is knowledge about relationship to authorities, to peers, and to those to whom the counselee is an authority or supervisor. These relationships are the kind of things that the pastor needs to pay attention to, learn about, and become comfortable talking about. In addition to that, again as we have noted before, the pastor's relational wisdom is expressed through being able to help the concerned person feel secure in talking about the problem; being sensitive to her feelings about it and being as simple, direct, and honest in talking about the problem as it is possible to be. In doing this, the quality of the relationship in discussing the problem is that of peers gaining something from each other in facing a situation together.

Another issue that often comes up in discussion of problems at work is how personal or expressive of her own feelings about the work situation the troubled person can afford to be. In virtually every work-related situation what must be dealt with is both function (is the job getting done) and feeling (the satisfaction or dissatisfaction of the persons involved in the job.) The pastor and his counselee need to be able to talk about both and in doing so empower the counselee to deal in some way with both at the work situation. Throughout the conversation the pastor is trying to avoid giving reassuring words without evidence that they are accurate or true while searching for ways of thinking and behaving in the counselee that can be used to point to strengths of which she is not sufficiently aware.

Work Problems within the Faith Community Itself

Consultation about a work problem or conflict within the faith community of which both the pastor and counselee are a part is different from other problems about work because in this situation the pastor has more of a stake in the outcome. In contrast to other problems in which the pastor has no stake in the outcome, in this one he is not just concerned with the person bringing the problem but he also has some responsibility for working toward a satisfactory solution to the problem. On the one hand, in dealing with the interpersonal conflicts or tensions in the situation, he can proceed as he might in any work situation in which the pastor has no responsibility. Because the pastor probably knows more about this troubling situation than he does about one in a setting in which he is not involved, he can make more use of the structures of the familiar community's organization to address the situation. In this situation he will make every effort to refer the problem to the responsible group within the community's structure in order that it be dealt with as something beyond the opinions of those involved in an interpersonal conflict.

Reflection and Conclusion

This chapter deals with some of the things that should happen in a second meeting for pastoral counseling with a pastor who is not trained in mental health counseling. Pastoral counseling is a continuation of the pastoral care that the pastor already knows something about within a structure that attempts to create dialogue about the problem presented and that attempts to place it within the larger contest of the troubled person's life. The pastor's concern is being present with the person seeking help in her lostness and offering companionship and some direction. A further concern present since the beginning of the first counseling conversation has to do with the possibility of referral. Can the person or persons get enough help from the pastor, or do they need assistance from someone the pastor knows about who has more specialized training dealing with the kind of problem presented? Should a referral take place, it will almost always be more effective because of what has happened in the relationship with the pastor. Moreover, the pastor will continue to be available to offer brief, supportive pastoral care to the persons he has referred to another helper. As was the case in the first counseling conversation, the pastor will reflect upon what has happened in this meeting, indicate his prayerful concern about it, and offer to pray with the persons present now if that seems appropriate. Any prayer that the pastor offers should be brief and simple and related to what has gone on in the counseling meeting.

The next chapter will be focused upon issues having to do with the family and family-like relationships: those within the present family that live together, the families of origin of the individual family members, and ways of thinking about those relationships and dealing with them. This includes making decisions about the optimal closeness and distance of persons who are in some way a part of the family. The pastor's concern with families is with all of their generations, past, present, and future and with the way the generations attempt to care or fail to care for each other at all stages of life. It is important that pastors value the experience that they already have with family issues, develop it further, and use it in counseling through the structure of family conferences with couples or with members of all generations of the family.

Chapter Four

Pastoral Consultation on Family and Family-Like Relationships

Just as pastors have a great deal of experience in dealing with loss and grief work in their regular care for the religious community they serve, most pastors also have a great deal of experience related to the life of families, their own and those of their parishioners. Pastors are experienced in providing ministry to families in baptism, confirmation, preparation for marriage, marriage, parent-child relationships, and the family life crises of grief and death. This experience provides an important part of their preparation for counseling with couples and families about marriage and family problems.

Consider, for example, what a pastor does in helping a couple prepare for their wedding. The couple actually marries themselves with the vows that they take. In deciding to get married they have already taken vows to each other privately. The pastor's role is to assist them in doing that publically in order to certify that their marriage has taken place. In preparation for that public commitment the pastor's role is to interpret those vows and their implications and to represent the religious community's support of the couple in this decision and action about their life together. Similar to what she does before and during a wedding, the pastor's counseling role with a couple or family is a consultative and supportive one. She does not make the decisions or carry out what has been decided. She is simply present, representing religious faith in supporting and guiding.

An important part of a pastor's work, in serving a community of faith or representing the religious dimension of life in a more secular community, is paying attention to and learning from family issues that emerge among the community's members. Certainly not all or not enough pastors do this, but one can argue that a significant part of a pastor's calling is to use the experience with families to study and cultivate her relational wisdom about families.

If the pastor can be aware that she is in familiar territory when asked to consult with a couple or family about a problem, she should also be aware of a proverb I heard from one of my teachers a long time ago when he was helping us to be prepared for oral exams: "Don't be so intimidated by what you don't know about a problem that you can't make use of what you do know." Thus, when invited, she needs to be available. At the same time she needs to remember that she's not a family therapist and her function is more to care than to cure. Her function with the couple or family is penultimate, to be present with the family pain and realize that her ministry is likely to involve referring them to someone else who can finish what the pastor has begun. Again, the pastor is not a family therapist and should not try to be one.

Thinking about the Family Generationally

A valuable part of thinking about the family that has been learned from professional family therapists is that family problems are seldom dealt with adequately within only one generation. It is important to think about and work with the couples and families as a system of relationships, not just working with the individual who is most aware of the problem. Because only one member of the family may have voiced the family's pain, and because it is more familiar and comfortable to talk with one person rather than more than one, the pastor will be tempted to respond to the marital or family crisis with a pastoral conversation with only one family member. Her responsibility, however, is to care for the whole family and, if the family is a member of the faith community that the pastor represents and serves, she has, at least implicitly, already been given permission to care actively for each member of the family system as well as to engage the whole group. Even if the family is not a member of the pastor's faith community, she should simply say that it is often helpful to meet for a conference with the couple or with all those in the household, and she should ask for permission to do that.

It is not merely the psychological wisdom of the family therapists that underscores the importance of dealing in some way with not only one member but with all the generations of the family. The Bible, particularly the Old Testament, reminds us that we are not merely individuals. We are persons who are a part of generations. Some of the most difficult public reading of the Bible comes in the recital of generations, as in "These are the generations of Abraham, Isaac, and Jacob." Although the recital of generations is dull prose, it is an important part of the commandment to honor our parents. It also places us among the generations of our family and reminds us of who we are. Whether or not we speak of this in specifically Christian terms, we are connected to each other, and that is a profound moral responsibility. To be a human being is to care for those who have come before, those in our own generation, and those who come after us as well as to care for ourselves.

Whenever they try to be helpful to a family, pastors inevitably represent what "ought" to be as well as what "is." A valuable part of that "ought" has to do with how the balances of care are worked out within and between the generations. The pastor's relational wisdom should include the knowledge that tensions involved in the care of one's generations and care for self and for one's significant other are always taking place in families. The pastor who has understood some of this is better able to engage a family in dialogue about their balances of care. That dialogue can in most cases help members of the family move in the direction of a more appropriate balance of care between themselves and the other generations of their family.

Pain in the relationship of a couple can seldom be separated from problems in the parent generation or in the generation of the children. Although a family may literally have more than three living generations, thinking generationally may be done adequately by using only three: the generation before; one's own generation; and the generation that comes after one's own. Certainly professional couple therapists can demonstrate and teach communication techniques that improve marital satisfaction within the couple's generation alone, but the most effective family consultation and care is usually related to something that was learned between at least two of the family's generations. This, for example, may have been when members of the couple were children themselves or as parental figures dealing with those dependent upon them. It is important that the pastor develop her relational wisdom by careful observation and reflection on the generations of particular families.

Thinking about the Family Normatively

Although most of a pastor's relational wisdom can come from experience as a pastor with persons in families and in family-like relationships, some attention to psychological theories about marriage and the family can be helpful. In pastoral counseling a pastor is dealing with the "is" more than the "ought," but it is important for the pastor to be continually developing her own view of what a relationship within one's own generation ought to be. In my own experience both as a pastor and as a professional counselor, three such theories have resonated strongly with a pastoral theological understanding of how a family, and particularly the marital couple within the family, ought to be (see John Patton, *Pastoral Care: An Essential Guide* [Nashville: Abingdon Press, 2005]).

Family therapists Lyman and Adele Wynne say that the closeness that is possible in the marriage relationship (and I believe in other significant same-generation relationships) is built upon a mutuality based upon three things: (1) the caretaking that takes place in a parent-child relationship, (2) a satisfactory conversational exchange of meanings and messages, and (3) joint problem-solving and the sharing of everyday tasks (Lyman Wynne and Adele Wynne, "The Quest for Intimacy," *Journal of Marital and Family Therapy* 12, no. 4 [1986]: 383–94). From a nonpastoral or theological perspective, the Wynnes are saying some of the things that a pastoral counselor needs to look for and pay attention to in thinking about what significant personal relationships between peers ought to involve.

Similarly, another social theorist, Peter Berger, writes of what a marriage ought to be in terms of persons developing a common world of meaning. He throws in a biblical reference in doing this and makes use of the book of Genesis and its picture of God's giving to humankind the task of naming the animals. He argues that this can be seen as a symbol of the human task of all of us in ordering the world in meaningful relationship to ourselves. An example of this can be seen in children when they begin to talk and name things in order to understand their relationship to them. On a different level, with adults the reality of our personal world is sustained through conversation with significant others. The "strength and continuity of significant relationships depends upon continually carrying on conversation about this world around us. The closeness and intimacy in a marriage relationship grows out of the construction of a common world of meaning through conversation" (Peter Berger, *Facing Up to Modernity: Excursions in Society, Politics, and Religion* [New York: Basic Books, 1977], 7–10).

Psychiatrists Thomas Malone and his son Patrick have also discussed closeness and intimacy within one's own generation in a way that can be useful to a pastor in understanding what is or is not going on in a marriage. They address the question, so often voiced in thoughts and conversation about a marriage, "How can I be myself when I am in relationship to another person?" by comparing and contrasting the meaning of the terms *closeness* and *intimacy*. Closeness is an experience in which I am more aware of the other person than I am of myself, more aware of his or her needs than I am my own. At best, the giving and receiving is balanced between the partners.

In contrast to closeness, intimacy is when a couple is together and both of them are more aware of themselves than they are of the other. Intimacy is when you can be in your own personal space and at the same time also be in the space you share with another. It is not that in intimate experience you are only aware of yourself and not the other. Rather in the experience of intimacy you experience yourself as being more of who you are in that relationship than when you are separated from it (Thomas Patrick Malone and Patrick Thomas Malone, *The Art of Intimacy* [New York: Prentice Hall Press, 1987], 23–29).

Marriages are maintained and strengthened by developing the ability to be both close and intimate. Both closeness (awareness of and response to the need of the other) and intimacy (experiencing one's self most fully when in the presence of the other) deepen our capacity to care for self and other in all of my generations. Making use of nonpastoral theories like these that supplement the pastoral thinking on marriage and the family can be useful in developing relational wisdom regarding what marriages ought to be.

Contributions from Premarital Consultation

Premarital consultation is discussed here because it is one of the places that pastors are involved in using a clearly defined structure in pastoral work with individuals and small groups. Pastors who chose to do no other type of counseling are accustomed to having premarital meetings with couples who ask them to perform their marriage ceremony. This familiarity can contribute to the pastor's being comfortable in using structure to facilitate her counseling with persons who may come to her with other marital or family concerns. I give a suggested structure for doing this in order to stir the pastor's thinking about what she usually does and why.

Some pastors perform weddings as a kind of private practice without any involvement of the church that ordained them. Others do this as a part of the ministry that the church offers in allowing the couple to use the sanctuary for the wedding. There are a lot of interesting practices and customs related to this as well as a lot of stories that pastors tell about the things that can happen before and after weddings they have been involved in.

There are two kinds of premarital work that the pastor does. The first is by far the most common. It is premarital consultation when the members of the couple acknowledge no particular concerns about their relationship. The couple comes to the pastor because the church in which they want to have the wedding requires a meeting with the pastor or because they or perhaps a family member thinks this kind of meeting is important to have. In that circumstance, in which they are not saying that they need help with something, the consultation does not meet the definition of counseling, which involves saying, "I or we have a problem and need help."

The second kind of premarital work occurs less frequently. Occasionally couples do ask for help with something in their relationship in the process of a consultation that was initially understood as the first type. With the couples who do ask for help, at least a portion of the meetings they have with the pastor may be conducted like any other meeting that focuses on a relational problem. The purpose of both kinds of premarital consultation is to encourage the couple to think about marriage, particularly their marriage, before they actually marry each other. It is to encourage them also to think about marriage after the wedding has happened and to make asking for help a less threatening thing to do.

I believe that the most useful structure for premarital consultation is one that focuses on the relationship within the families from which members of the couple come, their families of origin. Couples who are not aware of any problem in their relationship or are not at the point of wanting to talk about it can much more easily reflect upon and comment on their parents' relationship or the relationship of other parental figures than they can discuss their own relationship.

I suggest getting a few more or less objective facts about where they are living, where they are working, where each one grew up, how they met, and what has been important to them in their lives so far. Then pastors should introduce the structure of the premarital consultation something like this or develop a comparable statement of their own, hopefully not in one long speech but if possible in dialogue with the couple.

> What I have found particularly useful to do in premarital conversations—and I usually think it is important for us to meet at least two, possibly three, times—is this: I want you to think with me about your families of origin. The first of these families, the one that we'll spend the most time with, is the

household you grew up in, your parents, your brothers and sisters, and any others who you lived with you while growing up. That family has influenced your understanding and hopes from marriage more than you know or acknowledge. We're going to spend most of the time on your earliest family influence—your family of origin. If either of you have had a marriage broken by divorce or death, we also need to spend at least some time talking together about that marriage and how you think that it has influenced the way you are in your life now.

Before we get into the specific things that are to be said and done in your wedding I want to talk with you about what we might call your faith family of origin. The reason you wanted a minister to perform your wedding ceremony or to have the wedding in a church suggests that something related to religion is important to you. Tell me about your faith family, the particular persons who have most influenced your values and religious convictions. Then we'll discuss the various elements in the traditional wedding service, where they come from and what they mean, and try to relate them to particular concerns you have about what should be in the service so that we can come up with a plan for this particular wedding.

There is no particular way the story of these two families of origin needs to be discussed. It usually begins with the "getting to know you" kind of questions about where each member of the couple grew up, what his or her parents did for a living, what they were like when both were younger. What about other significant adults, brothers and sisters, good friends, and so on—the kind of things you may already know about parishioners but need to find out about others. Then there are questions about family financial resources, differences of the parents in handling money and showing affection for each other. Did the family members touch each other or keep their distance? Were there family crises, significant deaths, illnesses, or other losses?

Get this kind of material from each member of the couple, and then ask them if they heard about anything that they hadn't heard before, and comment that some of these things are important for them to know about and remember. Virtually all of the first session should be spent on family-of-origin material, with the pastor commenting on how important those stories are in influencing the couple's present relationship. There may be other things that the pastor feels are important to discuss or do, but trying to reflect on families of origin has, in my experience, been most important.

The second session should begin with a question about what each one remembers about the previous session and any conversations the couple has had that seemingly grew out of their meeting with the pastor. Depending upon what kind of response to this there is, this may be a good time to indicate that the pastor can make time to talk more about this if they would like to do that. One of the major values of premarital consultation is to let the participants experience some of value of talking to a pastor about their lives.

Then go on to the faith family. Talk about this in terms of their religious history or lack of it and the values in life that are important to them; note similarities and differences in this. How did their parents deal with value and religious differences? The concern here is not to get far into the discussion of religion itself but to note similarities and differences in the way the couple views what is most important in life. It is probably a good time to bring in the value or importance to them of having children or not having them, indicating how important it is for them to have some agreement about this as well as accepting differences in values between them.

A discussion of the elements in the wedding service comes naturally after the faith family discussion. The pastor will probably have worked out any significant differences between her and the couple in the initial conversation in which an agreement about performing the marriage ceremony was made. At this point in their conversations the pastor is attempting to acquaint the couple with the religious community that is helping them to marry each other. This context is contributing to the vows they make and the statements about marriage that compose the marriage service. The pastor might conclude by saying something like this: "That's what the ceremony we'll be participating in is saying about marriage. Is this an honest statement about how you are understanding what marriage is for you?"

If the couple and the pastor have significant common agreement about what marriage is for them, they go on to a final summary of their meeting. The pastor should point out strengths and possible problems or tensions that they bring to the marriage and indicate that after the wedding, if there are things that they would like to talk about with her, she'll be glad to do this or can refer them to a competent couples' counselor. If a referral is made, it should be done in a way that suggests that getting help somewhere along the way is not a disaster but a normal and helpful thing to do and that the pastor's primary concern is to be a transition figure who can help them along the way to getting some assistance.

The importance of premarital consultation, whether or not there is a conscious awareness of problems or potential problems, is not in its offering useful information about finances, in-laws, potential conflicts between work and family, sex, and the decision to have children or not. Its importance is in helping to establish a pattern of the couple's talking about their marriage and how they feel about it. If they have done this before the marriage, they are more likely to be able to do this later on in the course of the marriage as well as to be able to ask for any needed help. As I suggested earlier, the familiarity of the pastor with premarital consultation can contribute to the pastor's being comfortable in using structure to facilitate her counseling with persons who may come to her with family problems.

Contributions from Group Theory and Experience

Just as the pastor's experience in structuring premarital consultation can contribute to her wisdom for providing an appropriate structure for counseling about family problems, so can knowledge and experience about groups and group leadership. Most pastors have a lot of experience in working with groups. This happens most often within the church or other community organizations in which the minister has a leadership role. Much of what occurs in those groups, when planned and reflected upon, is experience that can contribute to the pastor's relational wisdom and thus to her counseling. There are many theories of group behavior and how to be an appropriate group leader. In my judgment the most useful features of a number of those theories is that all groups have two basic needs: (1) to accomplish a stated task, usually the group's stated reason for meeting; and (2) to offer emotional satisfaction to its members, contributing to their feeling better about themselves.

The pastor who is developing and using her relational wisdom should be constantly aware of these two needs and structure meetings with the groups she leads and those with individuals so that a sense of accomplishing a task and the sense of personal recognition and emotional satisfaction are achieved by its individual members. Accomplishing the group's stated reason for meeting or making some progress toward that goal that the members can experience is necessary both in regularly scheduled group meetings and in pastoral counseling. In the latter, for example, although something else may emerge as more important, it is essential that some progress be achieved toward dealing in some way with the first presented problem.

Then, in virtually all of the groups for which the pastor has responsibility, the members need to get something personal out of them. Usually that is the satisfaction of being heard and understood by another person or persons and having what one has said seem to be valued and used to accomplish the task of the meeting. The pastor learns or needs to learn very quickly that you can't spend all of the group's or a counselee's time in either accomplishing the stated agenda or in letting particularly emotionally needy persons express themselves without limits. Group observation, study, and practice can be a major contributor to the pastor's relational wisdom for counseling.

Beginning Consultation about Problems in the Family

One of the most familiar family problems that pastors hear about is one that may be first expressed something like this: "My husband works all the time. He never seems to be a part of the family." If the pastor is a careful listener, she will have noticed that the first statement of the problem is loaded with expressions of feeling about what is presented as a simple description of fact. "All the time" is almost undoubtedly an extravagant statement or figure of speech not intended to be taken literally but to express feeling. It is a way that persons can convey their feelings without explicitly acknowledging them.

In contrast to this indirect mode of speech, the pastor's concern should be to get the counselee to express her feelings or pain about what is happening in her life rather than to tell the pastor what is wrong with her husband. That's usually not easy to do, but when it can be done there will probably be enough relief in feeling heard and understood to enable the counselee to develop some initiative to improve the situation.

In order to encourage the expression of the counselee's own feelings, the pastor might respond to the complaint about the husband by saying,

> That sounds like it's really difficult to deal with. Could you say more about the kind of feelings it stirs up in you?

Usually the troubled person cannot respond to a question focused on her feelings the first time it is asked, so the pastor tries one more time at this point in the conversation.

> It may seem obvious that I would know how you feel about a situation like this. I feel sure that you may be angry or hurt or something else, but it would help me to understand if you could tell me.

Sometimes the pastor may get a response to that, but quite often she will not, so she simply makes a mental note of that and decides to come back with an attempt to get a direct expression of feelings later on. In leaving the question about feelings, the pastor's best second choice of what to do is to ask for a specific situation that illustrates what the counselee is describing,

> What do you remember about the last time that happened?

Asking for description of a specific event is a way of getting away from abstractions to a picture, something to which one might give a specific response such as,

> It must have hurt a lot to have your feelings ignored in that way.

The pastor is guessing here based on her past experience, but it's a reasonable guess and one that may elicit a direct expression of feelings.

The pastor is trying in this instance to develop a relationship in which the person seeking help can express what she feels about her life right now. She and the pastor are talking about a problem she has with her husband, but at the same time they are talking about what she is feeling about her life. The goal of counseling as a part of pastoral care is to get the counselee's feelings about life into the room so that the parties in the conversation are not dealing with a problem or a person "out there" somewhere but are sharing some of the pain and discouragement of one of them about where she is in her life. That doesn't change the husband's behavior, but it offers a supportive response to this woman's feeling of lostness and can also offer her a sense that someone is with her in thinking about what is possible for her to do about the pain in her life.

It is important to note two things going on in this conversation about the wife's feeling of pain and discouragement in her marriage. In response to the fact that the problem is described as having to do with the marriage, it is important that the pastor ask about the possibility that the husband might come to the next session so that the three of them can have a family conference. Such a meeting may be therapeutic in a sense, but it is important for the pastor and those who meet with her not to think of it as therapy. It can indeed pave the way for a good referral for such therapy, but it serves primarily as a way to get the family pain discussed more openly and to help the couple acknowledge need for further help.

It should be noted here that if the person seeking help mentioned a problem related to the family in the first inquiry about pastoral counseling, the pastor should have raised the question about both members of the couple coming to see her together. As a pastor, not a family therapist, she is not in position to insist on that, but it should be suggested as something useful as early as possible. I will discuss a way of structuring a family conference later in the chapter. Here the pastor is paving the way for a referral to one who is recognized as a marriage and family therapist. Moreover, the fact that the pastor has met with the couple in a setting where they could go over the problem with a third person will make it much more likely that the referral will go well than if the pastor quickly tried to hurry the couple off to the professional therapist. Her meeting with the couple has conveyed in some way that it's OK to discuss having marriage problems with a person who can understand them from an unbiased point of view.

The wife's expression of her feelings to the pastor is the beginning of the wife learning that it is in a secure and trusted relationship in which a lot of people get help, whether in pastoral care or professional psychotherapy. This gives her the experience of being reconnected to at least one understanding person during a personal time of lostness. The time-limited counseling that the pastor offers can be enough for this to take place, or if the person is a member of a church or community in which both she and the pastor are a part, the relationship can be further strengthened through other relationships there. If she is referred with or without her partner to a mental health professional, she will be better equipped to use that relationship because of her prior positive experience in relationship.

In the type of situation described above, the pastor has encouraged the woman whom she has seen for one conversation to ask her husband to come to counseling with her for their next meeting. It is important for the pastor to leave it to the wife to ask her husband to come. If she says to the pastor, "I think he's more likely to come if you call and ask him," the pastor should decline to do so because this is taking the initiative to come for help away from the family unit needing it and encouraging the wife's feeling of helplessness. Rather, she responds to her request by saying something like this, "I think it is important for you to ask him to come and for you to try to convey the importance of this to you. I believe that will help you in the long run." The person or family who asks for help is more likely to get it than the one who comes because someone else in the family thought they needed it.

If the husband decides not come to the second pastoral counseling meeting there are three things that should take place in the meeting with his wife: (1) the pastor continues to dialogue with her about what she is feeling rather than what's wrong with her husband; (2) as discussed in chapter 3, the pastor tries to expand the frame of the conversation so they are also talking about this person's life, not just her marriage; and (3) the pastor either realizes that they are not to have more than one more meeting for counseling at this time, so there should be a plan for referral to a professional counselor or the pastor creates the option of coming back for a follow-up visit in a month or six weeks from now.

It is difficult for some pastors to set limits on their time with a particular person, but it is important to do so. Setting such limits is easier to do if the pastor has an understanding with a committee of the church or institution in which she serves that her counseling ministry is limited to three, not more than four, meetings with a person. Although a person who has received counseling may come back on an infrequent basis to talk about where her life is now, it is understood that the pastor will not enter into long-term counseling relationships in this setting for ministry. Moreover, because the pastoral care ministry, including pastoral counseling, involves responding sensitively to persons' feelings, it is too easy for the pastor to become a substitute for the unsatisfactory family relationship. That is natural and all right in a crisis and on a temporary basis. In one sense that's what pastoral care is, but having long-term special relationships to some members of the community and not others is inappropriate and potentially destructive to the pastor's relationship with the whole community.

What Should Be Done in Pastoral Consultation with a Family

There are three things that should be done in the family counseling conversation whether it is with the wife alone or with the couple or family. As we noted above, the first is the pastor's continuing encouragement of each person to talk to her in ways that focus on what that person is feeling. When the counselee tells the pastor about something that has happened, the pastor's concern should be more upon how the teller of the story felt about it than upon the details of what happened. As was noted in an earlier chapter, a man who is not used to talking about his feelings and has difficulty in doing it can often want the person to whom he's telling the story to know what he was feeling without his having to express those feelings. If the pastor can encourage the person to express what's going on with him rather than expecting the pastor to know, something important for his life will have already taken place, namely the satisfaction of experiencing a caring relationship. This is something that takes place both in good mental health counseling and in good pastoral care.

The second thing that should happen in the conversation is talking about life, not just about the immediate problem. Talking about life and its meaning is a significant part of what a minister is about in preaching, teaching, and in ordinary but not so ordinary conversations with persons in her broader ministry. What she is doing in counseling conversation is more of that. The marriage problem will be solved or not solved, but whatever the case, life will go on.

Talking about one's relationships and life's goals and values is something most people need some practice doing. That's what needs to go on in addition to dealing with the present problem with the marriage or family. The pastor might say, "Tell me a little more about your life and what's been important to you over the years. That will help me in understanding how you're feeling now." There are many different ways of trying to convey that the pastor is concerned with the person and not just the problem, and most of them can lead into the counselees talking about themselves and what they hope for in life, their disappointments, and, sometimes, their feelings of failure. Letting a caring person know about these things and appreciate who he is can be helpful in living through the difficult time he is having now. Also a part of asking about the larger view of this person's life is discussing what the counselee hopes for in the future. Although what is being emphasized here is the structure for understanding a life and a problem through questions and dialogue, underlying all is "care-full" listening to what is said by the counselee and the pastor's response to what she has heard.

The third thing that should happen, usually toward the end of the time allotted for the meeting, is that the pastor should respond in ways similar to what was said about ending meetings earlier in the book. She should offer a brief summary of what she has heard with an assessment of the positive and negative things noted in the relationship and end with the question of whether or not the persons present want to meet for another conversation. Or, on the basis of what the pastor has heard, she may want to say that it sounds to her like the persons have more going on than they have time to deal with, and that she would like to refer them to a professional counselor who spends most or all of his or her time in doing psychotherapy. Any way that referral can be made more personal in the sense of knowing the person or the person's work to whom the counselee is being referred can make it more likely that the connection with the professional therapist will occur.

If the husband has come in with his wife, the counseling conversation becomes a family conference, one that is similar to what happens if the pastor is able to meet with other members of the family as well as with the couple. The situation we are discussing here is one in which one member of the family has come in first and then one or more come later. Should it work out that both members of the couple come into the first meeting together, the suggestion for the structure of the meeting is something like this. Again, we pick up a few things that have been said earlier.

The pastor says, "I'm glad both of you were able to come today." And then she mentions any conversations she has had with any one of them before this meeting. "I was talking to Jane at the end of our previous meeting, and she said that she had some concerns about what was going on in the family right now. I suggested that both of you come in so that all of us could talk about it together." If any other conversations took place prior to this meeting, they should also be mentioned so that no two persons have a connection that is not mentioned here at the beginning.

An advantage of this family conference structure for pastoral counseling is that it is in some useful ways similar to what the pastor does in leading or influencing what goes on in working with other kinds of groups in the church. Her goal there is also to facilitate persons expressing themselves personally and being able to hear each other. The similarity between these two types of groups makes pastoral conversations about life and family problems more like what the pastor does in her other work in ministry. Counseling structured in this way is not so different, and this in fact makes the pastor better prepared for counseling than it may seem to her that she is. To use the biblical metaphor, the care of the whole flock can contribute to the search for the lost sheep. Each type of ministry has the possibility of reenforcing the effectiveness of the other and of continuing to develop the pastor's relational wisdom. Counseling may not be a major part of her entire ministry, but the relational understanding and practice of it can contribute to all that the pastor does.

The basic structure for the meeting is this: Each member of the family who is present (and this is the case if only the couple is there and also if there are other family members there) is asked to talk to the pastor (the family outsider) about what he or she sees is wrong with or painful in the family's present situation and express how he or she feels about it. The goal is to have both what hurts and the feelings about that expressed by each one.

When the pastor begins the conference, and in order to make it clear that she is in charge of the way the meeting will be conducted, she should be the one who in fact begins it. If both members of the couple are meeting with the pastor for the first time, the pastor usually should start the conversation with the person who contacted her about the counseling by simply telling the person who was not there about the circumstances of that conversation. For example the pastor might say,

> Jim, after the meeting of the Family Council last week Jane approached me and said that she would like to talk to me about a problem that related to your family. She didn't say what the problem was, but when she mentioned the family, I suggested that she talk with you about coming with her. I'm going to ask her to tell me about the problem from her point of view, and then I'll ask you to tell me about how you understand what she is describing. Jane, tell me what's troubling you about what's happening in the family now.

If for some reason Jim breaks in to "correct" Jane on the way she tells her story, the pastor quietly but firmly interrupts him by saying, "I want to hear from Jane first and then try to give equal time to you. What each of you remembers and feels about the situation is more important than trying right now to get agreement on the details of what has happened."

One of the things the pastor wants to avoid is having the couple get into the family conflict at the time scheduled for the family conference and in the process leave the pastor out of the discussion. What she is intending to do, and needs to do in order for the conference to be as useful as possible, is to get each member of the couple to talk primarily to her with the other member listening. In order to do this, the pastor needs to be firm in carrying out the way that the conference is conducted.

Let's suppose that Jane says, "Jim works all the time. We never have any time together." That certainly identifies a problem, but it's too general and a bit too abstract to understand the particular things that are bothering Jane. So the pastor might simply say, "Tell me a little more about that." The pastor doesn't complain about the generalities in the statement of the problem but asks for more detail to fill in the picture. "What's a particular time you remember that really bothered you?"

Jane tells of an incident in which it seems that because of Jim's single-minded concern with his job she was forgotten about or apparently ignored. The pastor comments on the hurt pain she must have felt with that. The pastor will need to use her own judgment about how long to stay with Jane and the story of her pain. Part of the structure of the conference is to go back to that, but now, rather than trying to get to Jim's memory of the painful moment that Jane recalled, the pastor asks Jim the same or similar question she posed to Jane, saying, "I want to go back to that incident that Jane remembers in a moment, but right now it's important to hear from you, Jim, about what seems to be difficult or painful in your relationship with Jane."

The reason for this question is because the purpose of the family conference is not so much to get the facts of the stories agreed upon as it is for everyone to hear what each person remembers and feels and to respond in a "care-full" listening and a pastoral way to them. In response to the question to Jim, two things may happen. Jim may say that Jane doesn't understand and appreciate how hard he has to work in order to get ahead. There's a good chance he won't say how he feels about that because to him it seems that his feelings about it should be obvious. On the other hand, the pastor is comfortable in using whatever wisdom she has about relationships to suggest that guessing or reading the mind of another person is seldom effective, and in a counseling conversation feelings need to be expressed out loud. So the pastor says, "I can guess how you feel about that, Jim, but it would help if you could tell me in your own words." If Jim can respond to that, things are already going well in the conference. If he just doesn't know how he feels or is too anxious to express his feelings, the pastor may give one of her guesses about Jim's feelings and ask whether or not that is right.

What has been attempted thus far in the meeting is hearing at least something of where each member of the couple experiences pain in the family and, hopefully, also an expression of their feelings about this. At this point there are two choices about what the pastor should do next: either to ask for another incident or story about family pain and feelings about it or to ask what each member of the couple heard in the other's story and feelings. The first purpose of the dialogue that the pastor is structuring is to offer an opportunity for each member of the couple to get the satisfaction of expressing his or her pain in the presence of the other without some defense or retaliation taking place. The pastor's purpose is to prevent retaliation from happening as well as to provide practice for the couple or family in hearing the other and letting the other persons know what has been heard. As a part of achieving both of these purposes the pastor will say what she has heard or felt in hearing the stories and feelings and check to see if either member of the couple heard things in the same way. These are things, by the way, that are not just useful in counseling but in the other dimensions of the pastor's work in the parish or other institution where her ministry takes place.

In doing this kind of couples or family consultation the pastor does not attempt to coach or control what is said but to structure the conversation so the each one has the best possible chance of hearing the other's hurt or pain and trying to understand it. If we reflect upon what has gone on in this structured meeting for couples or family counseling, we can see it as an attempt to convey or test the idea that family problems can be talked about in a constructive and helpful way with plans made for improving things. The role of the pastor, as one who represents relational wisdom, is to structure the way that those problems are discussed so that everyone is heard and, insofar as possible, understood. The pastor attempts to be an interpreter and clarifier. Her business is not to provide a particular solution to the problem, but her manner of discussing the problem is intended to convey the message that "You are not helpless to deal with this. You can do something yourselves to make it better, and I'll do my best to guide you in that or refer you to someone who may be able to help you more."

Chapter Five

On Consulting about Family-Type Problems

This final chapter discusses further use of pastoral authority in pastoral counseling with family and family-like problems and in relation to situations in which care often involves setting limits, expressing an unpopular opinion, or in some way or another saying "no" to a request for help. Limits were briefly mentioned earlier in the discussion of how the pastor structures meetings for pastoral counseling. In that discussion pastoral authority is addressed primarily in the pastor's insistence on how the counseling conversations should be conducted, not so much in dealing with the content of the conversations. In the following chapter I discussed how the pastor's authority may need to be used in dealing not just with the structure of the counseling but sometimes with the content of a problem where some action is needed. The choice of problems to discuss here is somewhat arbitrary, but those to be dealt with are: the abuse of self or others through addiction or physical, sexual, or emotional abuse; working out the balance between work life and family life; family-like relationships in other areas of life; young or middle-adult relationships with their aging parents; learning to be a peer and to offer peership to others; and family decision making on questions of life and death.

More on the Use of the Family Conference

Because the pastor is not a skilled psychotherapist, he needs more of a plan for the meeting and to stay responsible for how the meeting is conducted. Being responsible for how the meeting is conducted does not mean that the pastor is responsible for taking over or solving the problem. His responsibility is for conducting the meeting in such a way that all participants, including himself as pastor, are most likely to hear each other.

The general principle for conducting a meeting like this is that the less training a person has in leading a group, the more structure is needed. The pastor has experience with the pastoral care of families in crisis and in the "care-full" listening that goes on in pastoral care. However, to consult with a family at the family's initiative in order to deal with some ongoing family pain or problem, a structure like this one is needed for the participants to work together on how to deal with the problems presented.

The participants first take time in the conference to focus upon the family's present pain or problem, with each person present listening to what each one has heard from the others about it. Then it's time to move on to the other questions to be addressed. Usually the most time is spent on the question of how the family and each member of the family is feeling now. What each person sees as the problem is discussed, but the pastor works hardest on getting each member of the couple or family to express how the problem is hurting him or her achieving what they hope for a satisfactory life.

In addition to identifying the problem and the way it is affecting each member of the couple or family, two other questions should be raised and responded to in this first family conference. They are:

What have you tried to do about the problem and how has that worked?

What thoughts do you have now about how you might make things better for you and the family in the future?

The purpose of both questions is to place responsibility in the hands of the family members, not the pastor, for thinking and action about what to do. The pastor is responsible for how the meeting is conducted but not what is done about the problem.

These questions are intended to recognize that the problem is not just something that is happening now. It has had a past, has a present, and will in some way be present in the future. Past, present, and future all require some thinking and action. Expressing feelings about the problem is important, but not enough. The pastor is concerned to help the couple or family group move toward some action to change things. The question about what has been thought or done in the past is important in realizing that the problem has not always been the same. At one time it was not present or not present enough to be painful enough to worry about. If it could change from then until now, it can probably change between now and some future time. Asking about the past is also a way to recognize that thought and action about a life situation is not something new. It is a strength that has been there and may be able to be activated in a more productive way now. There may be reason to express some regret about some things done in the past, but the focus on regret should be a passing one that is aimed at going on in the future, having learned from past failures.

The question about future plans continues the theme established in discussing the past efforts to deal with the problem. It conveys the idea that something can be done even though it is unlikely that things can go back to the way they were before a painful situation or problem was recognized. In this first pastoral conversation about the problem, it is not expected that any thoughts as to what should be done are in any way a final decision about action. The purpose is to recognize that there is some kind of manageable future and to begin thinking about it together. Although the question is about the future is raised with each member of the couple or family individually, it implicitly raises a question about the future of the family constellation: in the light of the present pain or problem, in what form will the family continue to exist?

Sometimes when the question about the future is raised, one or both members of the couple will have begun thinking about future plans that don't include their spouse. Those plans may or may not be brought up at this time, and it is not the pastor's business to get into that during a first family conference. Here the intent is simply to identify that thinking about the future of the family is something on which the couple need to have a continuing commitment to work together. If they do not have that commitment, they may need to think of getting further help in moving on alone. In either case where the commitment is not present, this is an appropriate time for the pastor to raise the question about the best way for them to get further help.

One of the most important things in this kind of family conference is that the pastor needs to get over any "saving the marriage" thoughts or feelings. The pastor should be content with the ministry of being present with the family pain now and being willing to refer the couple to an experienced marriage and family therapist that the pastor knows. The pastor makes the referral to another because he is not qualified as a therapist and because working toward a satisfactory resolution of the problem will take longer than it is possible for a nonspecialist to do. Certainly, the pastor may offer to see the couple or family one more time or to see one member of the family about a particular concern, but it should be clearly understood that this is a finishing off and moving on to another kind of meeting, one that affirms the pastor's continuing relationship to this family, but not as a therapist. This can often be a way of helping marital or family therapy take place more effectively.

A family conference conducted by a pastor is a support and encouragement to each member of the family because it encourages the expression of their concerns. One thing repeatedly heard both from members of the marital pair or the children is that they don't feel heard by significant others in the family. The family conference structure can encourage this, particularly when the pastor maintains a focus on hearing the person more than trying to be the one to solve the problem. The problem may be solved in some way, but what the pastor works hardest at is helping each person feel heard, first by the pastor and then helping the other family members to hear each other. That's not an easy task, but sticking with a structure is usually helpful in getting some tension relief in the couple's relationship or in the family as a whole.

Underlying this concern to facilitate the verbal expression of feelings in the presence of other members of the family is the awareness of how much easier it is for many persons to express their feelings in actions rather than in words. Knowing the various psychological labels for this is not necessary. What is necessary is the pastor's effort to help the members of the family to talk to each other, using the structure of the family conference to do this.

There are two parts to this structure. The first is the one we have described before in which each member of the family who is present is asked to tell the pastor about his or her experience of pain or trouble in the family. Then after hearing from each one, the pastor goes back over the process asking them what each one has heard from the others. That beginning focus on the pain is followed by a question about what each has tried previously to deal with the pain. Then ask each family member present his or her thoughts about what should be done in the future. Each section of this structure is followed by questions about what each person has heard.

The second part of the family conference structure, whether with a couple or an entire family, is not second sequentially but is a part of what happens in the family conference from the beginning. The pastor insists that each member of the family responds to the questions the pastor asks, without responding at this time to the other members of the family. The goal of this part of the structure is that each member of the couple or family hears and tries to understand the other person's present. If they are not able to do that, at least the pastor has conveyed through the use of this simple structure the importance of doing this.

Another important part of insisting that family members respond to the pastor rather than to each other is that this has at least the possibility of breaking up the most familiar, unsatisfactory couple or family interaction pattern or family fight. In encouraging the expression of feelings, both positive and negative, the pastor risks encouraging the hurt that words can sometimes produce. If the pastor insists on staying in control of the structure, it is worth the risk. If the couple or family can't participate in responding to the structure, it is time for the pastor to consider saying two things,

> I don't think it helps for you to express your anger directly to each other while you're here. To express it to me in a place where it is safe for the other to hear is OK, but I have to insist that that's what should go on.
>
>   And it's important that you don't try to punish any other family member for what is said here after you leave.

And then, if in fact it seems that way to the pastor, he should say something like this,

> It appears to me that we are not able to work on this family pain or problem together, so what I want to do is to suggest a professional family therapist, whom I know, for you to see about what's troubling you.

What Has Been Going On in the Family Conference?

In thinking back over what is going on in the family conference, the pastor is using a structure, a form not unlike an agenda of a meeting, to encourage but contain uncomfortable and painful feelings within the family group. As in an official meeting of a group within a church or people-helping agency, the structure is used to encourage expression of personal feelings but also to keep them within limits, so that the participants can feel that it is reasonably safe to express them.

The purpose of this structured self-expression is to encourage the couple or family members to express their concerns in a more feeling way to each other and to try to understand the feelings of each person. The concern to facilitate expression of feelings and understanding in words is to head off the expression of those feelings in behavior that is more hurtful than words. The family conference emphasizes self-expression that is contained and controlled. If the self-expression in the group cannot seem to be contained within reasonable limits, it is time for the pastor to acknowledge the boundary and suggest referral to a particular professional mental health professional.

The family conference offers an example of listening and being heard that the family members are encouraged to imitate in their own way. Things are said by each person present, and then each family member is asked to report what he or she heard the other person say or what he or she noticed. The couple or family group is encouraged to pay attention and attempt to understand and take seriously what each other person is expressing. The pastor is helping the family develop listening skills by example. The real purpose of this focus on communication skills is to develop or recover trust in the relationships within the family.

It should be said again that all of the problems discussed in this chapter may need to be referred to another helping person. Problems need to be dealt with but not necessarily carried to a satisfactory resolution by the pastor. A satisfactory resolution of the problem is more likely, however, if the person or family is encouraged by a caring pastor to get further help.

In order to be effective, not just in pastoral counseling but in other dimensions of ministry, the pastor should read and study to develop more theoretical knowledge to go with a practical knowledge of relationships. There are some useful references in the back of this book. There are also many continuing education workshops for professional counselors and marriage and family therapists as well as workshops on group leadership that may be helpful for pastors. In making use of this education, the pastor should be aware that training and experience in ministry brings with it more useful experience and potential wisdom than that of many of the counselors who attend workshops on relationships are likely to have. What the pastor most has to offer is a practical kind of relational wisdom, much of which is relevant not just for counseling but for most of the leadership activities that the pastor has responsibility for in the church or other institution in which he serves.

Balancing between Work and Family

Most pastors with any significant amount of experience in life and ministry have heard a number of variations on this problem. It may have to do primarily with how much time one spouse spends with his or her primary job versus how much time (and type of time) spent with the marriage partner and other family members. As has already been suggested in the structure for a family conference, the pastor's task, if he is consulted about this, is to facilitate their talking about the problem, first with the pastor and then with each other.

The pastor begins the counseling process by asking to hear the feelings of the person most aware of the problem. This is not simply a matter of encouraging that person to ventilate her feelings because doing that too often results in blaming other persons rather than expressing what she herself feels. The pastor needs to become comfortable in noticing, understanding, and pointing out the difference between those two things. That is why the structuring we have discussed earlier is so important.

As the pastor insists on hearing how the person speaking is feeling, he needs to guard against getting hooked into commenting—at least at this time—on any abstract discussion of what is right and wrong about the behavior discussed. Although pastors represent a concern for right and wrong, getting caught in an abstract discussion about that can take the marriage partners away from the present concern of communicating with each other about their feelings. When leading this kind of discussion, the pastor listens and responds to what he is hearing and attempts to assist in the understanding of the feelings of those involved.

When some understanding of feelings seems to have been achieved, the pastor asks about how what each member of the couple has proposed to do fits with the proposal of the other. He then encourages them to try these change proposals for a brief period of time before coming back for another meeting with him to discuss in what way their situation may have improved. He may also say that he can assist them in a referral to a marriage and family therapist if they seem ready to go farther in dealing with the problem. In all that he does, the pastor is attempting to support the couple or family in recognizing the importance of dealing with their relational problems and affirming the possibility of their doing that successfully if they choose to do so. He may also suggest some written resources on family relationships for them to read and possibly return to discuss with him. (See for example John M. Gottman, *The Relationship Cure: A 5 Step Guide to Strengthening Your Marriage, Family, and Friendships* [New York: Harmony Books, 2001].)

There are many variations in the struggle to balance marriage or family responsibilities with personal achievement goals. Only a few of them can be touched on here. Growing out of the cultural background and experience in the families of origin each person has goals that he or she wants or is expected to achieve, or there may be conflict between the couple because one of them seems to have no goals for improvement or very limited ones. The couple may be very much aware of their differences in commitment to goals or those differences may need to be brought into greater awareness and discussed.

The things we have discussed here are the kinds of things that should be discussed in most premarital preparation or counseling. Some of the most common personal goals are becoming a parent, achieving financial success, receiving recognition by others for one's achievement or service, and so on. Any of these can conflict with the relational needs of each member of the marital couple. Certainly there can be pride in the achievement or recognition of one's spouse but hurt in it as well, when one member of the couple appears to be seen as just an attachment to the other. These are the things that pastors who are constantly dealing with personal relationships in one way or another should be at home assisting others in talking about. The minister's task in pastoral counseling is guiding the discussion of these issues and providing a model for the couple or family to discuss them on their own and make plans for any necessary change.

Family-Like Problems at Work

One of the most familiar problems a pastor may be called upon to deal with is one that is occurring in the workplace, but the person experiences it as replicating some of the features of his family of origin. That family provides the first class for learning about life and how to get along in it. In the family we learn what to do to get our needs taken care of, how to do things that contribute to the family's life together, and how to become a leader or someone who is in charge of the task to be done. We learn these things to different degrees and in different ways, but the family provides us with experience in *being dependent* as a young child, in *becoming a peer* in various activities of the group, and in *developing the ability to lead* or to be the director of what's going on.

Those three relationships, of *dependency,* of *peership,* and of *leadership,* are present in much of our life experience, and it can be useful for the pastor to think of problems in life and work in terms of them. This certainly includes problems in the church that he has some responsibility for addressing. Education in the context of the workplace is constantly dealing with them. How is a particular person performing at her job, and what are the best ways to assist her in improving her performance? The clinical pastoral education that many pastors receive provides experience under supervision in all three of these basic relationships that can guide them in their attempts to help persons in their care learn from the parallels between work and family life.

This is something of what the pastor does in pastoral counseling with persons who talk with him about problems at work. The steps in that process are usually something like this: The pastor begins as usual with the question about what's bothering the person and how that makes the counselee feel. He listens carefully to what's being said, thinking about how one or more of the three basic relationships are involved and then says something like this: "I want to think with you about how this may or may not relate to your earlier life experience with the family you grew up in and your earlier work experience outside the home." The skill involved in doing this is being able to expand the frame of what's being talked about without getting too far away from the problem that was presented.

It is important to recognize the potential parallels and contrasts in all human interpersonal experience and the value of the parallels between the pastor's own earlier experience and the situation being described to him. This can stir the humanness the pastor can share in relationship with the counselee, but if he shares too much of his own story it can get in the way and dominate what is being discussed. What the pastor can use are the feelings the person's story stirs in him in order to respond to it more sensitively in the context of the counselee's story.

What the pastor is going to do in relation to the problem the counselee has presented is to suggest the possible influence of those parallel work and family relationships on what's going on. His method of doing this is not to get too smart and claim to know just what's going on. The pastor's concern is in getting the counselee to think about what he knows about his way of dealing with authorities, with peers, and with those accountable to him and to note parallels between past and present relationships.

Another element in this work-related counseling both for the counselee and the pastor in his own work in church or other institution is being aware of the dual needs of persons to accomplish a task and to achieve personal or emotional satisfaction. How are these related in what's troubling at work? How much of the problem involves the facts of what needs to be accomplished and how much is related to the personal needs of those involved? Talking about those things in the counseling session can help relieve some of the tension being experienced and leave the counselee freer to develop a plan of action for dealing with the issue. This is something that the pastor can support her in and consult with her about during a counseling meeting.

The discussion in this section of the chapter should suggest how often a pastor is called upon to deal with family-type relationships and how important it can be for him to continue to read, reflect on, and learn from that experience and to take seriously the relational wisdom he is developing. The steps in the counseling experience are similar to those that have already been discussed. Identify the problem that is presented. Insist on hearing the feelings about it, not just the problem. The pastor is not dealing with the problem apart from the person; therefore, what he is trying to do is help them have a more satisfactory experience and understanding of themself and of the situation they are dealing with.

Achieving an Adult–Adult Relationship with Parents

Being aware of the influence of the three basic human relationships learned in the family can contribute to dealing with another problem that pastors are often called upon to address: young or middle adults develop-ing an adult-adult relationship with their parents or with those who have been parental persons for them. As we have noted, all persons have some experience in dealing with these relationships, and this experience is some-thing the pastor can use in their counseling.

One mark of maturity or successful living is to be able to function effectively in all three of these basic relationships at every stage in adult life—to be dependent, a peer, and a leader or parental type of person. The oldest child, for example, is a peer among her siblings, but more than that she learns to take charge and function as the leader of the group. This can be satisfying up to a point, but what appears to be more satisfying, not just to the oldest but to the middle and youngest children as well, is to have experience in all three roles and functions and to develop the ability to move among them without getting stuck in one or another.

Most pastors have had the experience of talking with young and mid-dle adults about their or their spouse's relationship to their parents, more often just one of the parents. The problem is often presented as the adult child's lack of time for the parent. In a counseling conversation about this the pastor should begin, as in other pastoral counseling, by asking the per-son to describe the problem and her feelings about it. After hearing and responding to this description of the present condition, the frame of look-ing at the problem should be expanded by asking about the past character of the relationship with some story or event that illustrates it.

The concept of expanding the frame of the conversation is important in counseling, and it is the primary thing the pastor will be modeling and then encouraging the adult-child to do in relationship with her parents. The goal to be achieved is reducing the pressure of parental demands on the time of adult children for them to be together as adults without re-peating their parent-child relationship. This means that the pastor's coun-selee, the adult-child, needs to do all that she can to develop interest in the parent's life beyond just parent talk. One of the things that pastors and church groups can do to facilitate this is having educational programs that include the topic, particularly for young adults, of "Becoming Acquainted with Your Parents as Adults, not just as Parents." In counseling, at whatever stage of adult life it occurs, the pastor needs to direct some of the conversation to assisting in this.

With respect to the adult-child's worrying about her parent's complaint of not spending enough time with them, the pastor needs to ask the counselee, in the light of her present life situation, what seems realistic as to the amount of time that can be spent with the parent. There is obviously no one answer to this. Deciding about it may also involve working insofar as possible with other siblings about what they can do.

The pastor and counselee discuss the plan, support the adult-child in discussing it with the parent or parents, and then look at trying it over a period of time that seems appropriate to the situation. The counselee may then come back to discuss what's worked out and what hasn't, discussing the feelings stirred up by complaints that the parent may have had about it and coming up with an alternate plan if necessary.

An ethical framework for the pastor's thinking about this and discussing it can be a three-generation responsibility for family living, namely that a person has the responsibility to care for the generation before her, her own generation, including herself, and for the generation after her. It is important to work and rework the balance of this responsibility and find ways to deal with the guilt resulting from the imperfection of that balance. The pastor's counsel for the counselee is that she should take this responsibility seriously but also remember that grace is present to deal with the limitations and failures involved trying to do this.

Problems Related to Addiction and Abuse

Abuse means literally, "to take away from use"—to misuse or mistreat and, perhaps, to injure. Our concern here, then, is with the misuse and mistreatment of persons, the abused persons and the abuser's abuse of the self. Much of what is discussed here involves alcohol and other addictive substances. They are addressed here because situations involving these substances most often come to the attention of a pastor when a person becomes abusive. It is important for the pastor to offer "care-full" listening to whoever has come for help, the abused or the abuser. In this situation the pain of the present is important, but the pattern revealed by the past may be even more important, particularly in understanding the need and making a case for referral to treatment. The ongoing care of the pastor is expressed by listening to the story of abuse and then confronting the abuser or the abused person with the fact that this has happened before and that the abuse is not to be minimized and denied. It must be addressed now with action or it will be repeated, and there may be serious or fatal consequences.

To be helpful to the one who is abusing or to the person being abused, the pastor must deal directly with the person or persons experiencing the problem and who have approached the pastor for help. The pastor cannot do anything second hand to or for someone who is not there. The pastor's task, as we have discussed before, is always to deal with the pain and action or lack of action of the person who is there for help. The pastor needs to use his authority to insist that the person talk about her own feelings and behavior and to support her in her choice and action to stop tolerating the abuse. With the other involved persons, the abuser of himself or others, the pastor's action is to emphasize that the abusing person do something to get help for himself and not talk in any great length about what or whom he may blame his abusive action upon.

The pastor should use his ability to say "no," to avoid listening to stories about the abuser's drinking behavior or successes and failures about stopping it. That can be done more effectively in a group meeting with other abusers who have already sought help. The pastor can be helpful in offering a limited amount of listening to the abuser's talking about his pain or loneliness. The pastor knows something about that, but he needs to recognize how little he knows about addictive behavior and not think that he is going to be the one who is ultimately going to be helpful in the abuser's dealing with it. In most cases the pastor needs quite early in the counseling to begin the process of trying to refer the abuser to the best available community resource for dealing with this problem.

The word *begin* is used here because the process will likely take some time. The pastor will probably want to say honestly that he is concerned about the abuse of self and probably others that the abuser's drinking behavior is causing and encourage him to talk to his spouse about it. He may also say that he should encourage her to get help for herself and other members of the family with a group, such as Al-Anon, which is for family members of abusers. The pastor needs to know about the kind of denial that is so prominent in abusing families; be firm in responses, and be ready to act in referring the abuser and family for treatment.

A pastor must know what resources for addiction treatment are available in the community. It can be very helpful for pastors to have some direct knowledge of Alcoholics Anonymous (AA), Narcotics Anonymous (NA), and other abuse-related twelve-step groups that are available. If there is a for-profit treatment facility in the community, the pastor should know something about that facility's practices. Do its ethics balance appropriately with its need for patients? What other community resources are available—such as social workers, psychologists, and psychiatrists—who are knowledgeable about groups for addiction-related problems? If the pastor is to refer as an appropriate expression of care, he needs to know what and to whom he is referring. The more referral is based on some personal knowledge of a person or persons to whom the referral is being made, the more likely it is that it can be effective.

The Abuse of Others

Secrecy about abuse has been strongly supported by the power of shame and has made exposure of the problem particularly difficult. Surely, anything so shameful could not possibly be true, particularly among members of a religious community. Nevertheless, child sexual abuse, for example, has a long history in American society. Until the ascendancy of psychology in the twentieth century, however, Americans failed to identify child victims of sexual abuse because such crimes were hidden. Disbelief that such behavior occurred and distrust of young victims marked the early legal opinions on the subject. Moreover, in the case of child victims, if pregnancy could not result, the sexual act was not perceived as a concern of the law. On the other hand, child victims were viewed as accomplices who required corroboration in some form, preferably a confession by the defendant. If family members continued to stand by the accused, it was virtually impossible to convict the perpetrator.

How does the pastor respond in counseling to a report of child sexual abuse? He responds first by thinking about it. His response might be essentially the same as the counselee's—"it's awful"—but he can be more helpful if he can avoid letting his feelings get in the way of the counselee's expressing hers. He also needs to have a way of thinking about the problem and helps the counselee to think about it before acting. Moreover, as we have said before, the pastor needs to lead from strength. The pastor knows about pain from situations of illness and grief and first must deal with the help-seeker's feelings and, perhaps, the pastor's own feelings, particularly if the pastor is shocked by what was disclosed. The counselee needs to tell the story as she knows it in the context of a trusting relationship, and the pastor needs to be fully present to her pain. The pastor needs to be aware that shame is terribly difficult to deal with, but the counselee also needs to know that beginning to address it rather than attempting to hide it can help.

It can be helpful if the pastor has consulted with a lawyer about the abuse laws in the state and what is necessary for addressing the abuse when it occurs within the family and outside it. The pastor should also know the limits of confidentiality and tell the person asking for help the requirement that he report abuse to the proper authorities. Pastors should recognize that a gender, race, or class that is in power tends to hold onto that power by not being able to see things any other way. It is important for pastors who offer pastoral counseling of victims to examine their premises and prejudices about violence and about sexuality, their life experience and deepest feelings about women and men, and their beliefs about parents and children and family life.

In a church or other institutional setting there should be a subcommittee of the institution's governing board that is responsible for the institution's counseling ministry. That committee should have discussed or referred to a lawyer for assistance in understanding the legal and ethical responsibilities of the pastor and church in the case of reported abuse.

Moreover, the pastor needs to find out upon discovery of the abuse what the counselee wants to do. In the case of child abuse, the counselee may need to talk with her pediatrician and use that resource for any other knowledge about what should be done. In order to help, the pastor needs to know something about abuse, be present to the counselee in her lostness about it, offering a dependable trustworthy relationship, and be ready to guide and support any appropriate action that she takes. Unless there is clear danger of immediate further abuse, the pastor should not take any precipitous action. The pastor works to stabilize the situation and yet works with all deliberate speed, attempting to help the person feel support in any appropriate action she decides to take. Most important is that the pastor not work in isolation and that the pastor has a plan for dealing with reports of abuse. It is important that the pastor make every effort to ask questions in a matter-of-fact, normal, respectful tone of voice. A pastor's calmness and professional attitude can ease the feelings of shame and secrecy and may make action that is not possible now be possible at some future time.

As a part of self-examination by pastors concerning attitudes and assumptions, the pastor should recall the kind of blaming of victims that occurs in both church and society in the insistence that abused persons forgive their abusers. The idea of forgiveness is so valued and applauded by the church that persons are blamed by themselves or others when they don't at least say that they forgive someone who has hurt or abused them. Forgiveness is misunderstood as much as it is valued.

Genuine forgiveness is not forgetting or in any way condoning what has been done. Nor is it absolving abusers of all responsibility for their actions. Most important to understand is that forgiveness is not a clear-cut, one-time decision. It is a discovery, the by-product of an ongoing healing process. Failure to forgive is not a failure of will but occurs because wounds have not yet healed. Rather than being something we do, forgiveness is something that happens as a sign of positive self-esteem, when we are no longer building our identity around something that happened in the past. Our injuries are just a part of who we are, but injuries do not define our whole being. When we realize that punishing the one who has hurt us does not heal us, forgiveness is putting to better use the energy once consumed by rage and resentment and moving on with life.

Family Decisions Related to Life Transitions and End of Life

Because I have had less direct experience in this area of consultation than with problems discussed earlier in the book, I have consulted books on clinical ethics including several noted in the bibliography. In writing this chapter, I have also consulted personally with a clinical ethicist on the faculty of a medical school, a professor of theological ethics in a seminary, and an experienced chaplain in a university hospital. It is important for the pastor who is asked to be present in situations like those described below to look for consultation and help beyond what he knows and what is available in this book.

Although consultation about health care transitions sometimes take place in a hospital or other institutional setting with health care professionals present, the pastor who has been asked to meet with an individual or family to discuss such things should make every effort to meet first with the family alone. That meeting is not unlike meetings with the family that we have previously discussed. It is also similar to a meeting with a family when a pastor has been asked to perform a funeral or memorial service. It is a time when he can become familiar or more familiar with the life story and significant relationships of the deceased or person in a health care crisis.

The pastor needs to learn as much as possible about the family's life together, the family story prior to the present situation, how family relationships are being experienced now, and how they understand the present medical situation of the patient. Acute illness, including terminal conditions, are disruptive of the patient's and family's life story. One of the things pastors can do is help the family incorporate the story of the illness, and perhaps of hospitalization, into a story they can identify with and use in their decisions. This meeting with the family is also a good time for the pastor to pray with and for the family about the decisions they may need to make.

It is important to recognize ways in which consultation on life transitions and health matters involves getting in touch with the life stories of persons present in the situation. It is also important to be on the lookout for the convictions and values that are involved. The pastor needs to become aware, as much as possible, of the family's convictions and values about life and health. At the same time he needs to be in touch with his own beliefs. Whether he is fully aware of them or not, these beliefs are involved in the way he thinks about persons facing life and health care decisions.

Some of the theological and ethical questions about health and life care issues that pastors may have to address are these: How does the pastor's belief that human beings were created to be related to God and to other persons affect how he chooses to live in the world? How do his views on human suffering and sin affect this? What is involved in a person's living a good life, and how is this related to the understanding and care of the weak, disabled, or disadvantaged and equality in the way that health care resources are allocated? What responsibility do we have in caring for God's creation beyond our immediate concern for a meaningful life for ourselves and for our families?

The attending physicians involved in discussing the patient's situation with the family are likely to be aware of most of the principles and values noted below. Although no treatment options are completely free from the possibility of hurting the patient, the message present in the Hippocratic oath for physicians, "Do no harm," is very likely to be part of the physician's thinking about the patient, along with the principle, "Always do what is in the patient's best interests." There is or should be a conviction about equality in treatment, treating patients without favoritism for one patient over another. There should also be some knowledge of how the availability and limitations of health care resources in the community may affect the patient. Those present in deciding what to do about the treatment of this patient are involved in the larger decision about the uses of those resources. How are this patient's needs to be compared to the need of other patients' use of limited health resources? Patients and families also need to be made aware of the value of palliative treatment and hospice care.

Of these questions, the one that the pastor, the patient, and his or her family, and the health care professionals involved in this particular patient's situation are all dealing with is "What is involved in living a good life or simply a life worth living?" There are different ways of framing an answer to that question. One is that a good life involves having the capability, vigor, and freedom to achieve one's purposes in life and to find meaning in what one has done and can do. The understanding of health and the good life should also take into account the degree of suffering and disability involved in life and the value of living a disabled life, one that has never been or can ever be fully functional. Thinking about these questions from a Christian perspective also involves the conviction that this life is not all there is.

Until recent years most ethical decisions about what should be done for the patient have appeared to be guided primarily by principles. More recently there has developed a type of medical ethics related more to the patient's and family's story than to the more general principles of patient care. Narrative ethics asks different kinds of questions than ethics based primarily on law, philosophy, or theology. It focuses on how we got to the current point before thinking about what should be done. It is based upon the conviction that moral responsibilities can be discovered in understanding the interpersonal relationships within a family. Stories or narratives shape a person's moral identity and assist in determining how a person with that identity would behave in the present circumstances. What action would fit the best possible outcome of the story?

Narrative ethicist Arthur Frank, who has written extensively on the importance of encouraging persons to tell the stories of their illness, has said that for those persons who usually don't speak easily of their lives eliciting the story of their illness can be a way of encouraging them to go on beyond the illness story to talk about the larger story of their lives and the values they hold. In discussing what needs to be done in critical health and life transition situations, Frank, has said that narrative ethics treats everyone—patients, families, and health care workers—as all needing to reorient their stories toward what all those involved can agree to as the most acceptable decision in the patient's present situation ("Narrative Ethics as Dialogical Story-Telling," in "Narrative Ethics: The Role of Stories in Bioethics," ed. Martha Montello, special issue, *Hastings Center Report* 44 [January–February 2014]: S16–S20). This type of narrative-related ethics resonates clearly with what pastors usually attempt to do in their care and counseling.

The ill person's needs have priority in these life and health decisions, but each participant in the discussion of what should be done needs to learn some of the story of the others in order to construct an outcome in which all can participate. This approach can avoid having one story or one way of proceeding override all the others. If the patient and family have written directives about what should be and not be done about her care, they should be reviewed and followed. Sometimes written directives are too general to deal with the patient's or family's present situation, and new decisions need to be made. Patients and their families need to be fully informed about possible treatments or the termination of those treatments.

Ethicist Larry Churchill has said that practicing ethics is not like finding universally correct answers in the back of a math book. Instead, it is more like muddling through, doing what is possible, and often trying to find the least harmful alternative in tragic situations ("Narrative Awareness in Ethics Consultations: The Consultant as Story-Maker," in "Narrative Ethics: The Role of Stories in Bioethics," ed. Martha Montello, special issue, *Hastings Center Report* 44 [January–February 2014]: S36–S39). In writing about these issues in the last chapter of his book *Medical Ethics and the Faith Factor* (Grand Rapids, MI: William B. Eerdmans, 2009), physician and clinical ethicist Robert D. Orr has affirmed what he as a Christian prays for in medical situations where difficult decisions are required. I paraphrase his words below.

I do not pray for "the answer." Instead, I pray for three things: guidance, wisdom, and peace. I pray for guidance because I want God to help me to be able to set aside personal, psychological, or social biases. I want the divine authority to take precedence in the reasoning process.

I then pray for wisdom. It is a truism that "good ethics begins with good facts." Facts in a given case should include an inquiry about the patient's own faith tradition and an exploration of documents, teachings, or precedents in that faith tradition that may bear on the situation at hand.

And I pray for peace. This is my personal barometer. I want the divine Spirit to give me a feeling of "unpeace" or even turmoil if I am moving in the wrong direction with my human assessment. I hope for "the peace that passes all understanding" if I am working within acceptable faith boundaries.

Guidance, wisdom, and peace. Sounds simple, perhaps even simplistic. But as I wrestle with the gray areas, and as I deal with conflicts, I find considerable comfort in these precepts that ensure that I am not alone.

Final Reflections on the Value of the Nonspecialist Pastoral Counselor

The purpose of this book has been to encourage parish ministers and institutional and military chaplains who have little or no specialized training in counseling and psychotherapy to do pastoral counseling in the setting for ministry in which they serve. Although such ministers are not qualified to do mental health counseling that is recognized by professional counseling organizations and state licensure, the pastoral counseling they do can contribute significantly both to life and health. Ministers are often the first stop of persons who have become aware that they need help. Their offer of a supportive relationship can encourage those who come to them to seek further help if that is needed.

I have written this book based on many years of experience in ministry, first as a parish minister and university minister, then as a hospital chaplain, a professional pastoral counselor and marriage and family therapist, and finally as full-time professor in a theological seminary. During my years of specializing in professional counseling and psychotherapy, I found that I was much more effective in working with my patients if they had had at least one meeting with a caring and understanding pastor. When I received a referral from certain pastors I knew that I was much more likely to be able to be helpful. These pastors knew and had confidence in me and I in them. A valuable part of a pastor's work is being a step in the right direction for getting help.

The book has intended to offer a way of thinking about pastoral counseling and directions for doing it. It has argued that although pastors are not specialists in particular types of mental health counseling, they are specialists in having wisdom about relationships. That relational wisdom comes from their theological training and experience in preaching and teaching about a God who has chosen to be in a caring relationship with us and who directs us to be in such relationships with each other. Certainly pastors who have learned to reflect upon and learn from their experience in ministry have more of this relational wisdom than those who have not been particularly concerned about doing this. Even so, all ministers need to be aware of the opportunity of learning about human relationships they have in the ordinary work of ministry.

The book has described pastoral counseling as a type of pastoral care and, therefore, simply an extension of something that the pastor already knows about. The pastor does in counseling essentially the same thing that he does in pastoral care through "care-full" listening. The only difference is, first of all, that the person who comes for counseling has taken the initiative to come rather than having the pastor or religious community reach out to him. Second, pastoral counseling done by a pastor who has limited training needs to be carefully structured in order to accomplish its purposes. Much of what this book as done has been to suggest ways of structuring pastoral counseling conversations.

One of the important things I have been trying to say in the book comes from the proverb I mentioned in chapter 4: "Don't be so intimidated by what you don't know about something that you can't make use of what you do know." Because of your experience as a pastor, you know more about caring conversations with persons than you think. Pastoral counseling is a structured expression of that, and I have encouraged you to think of it in that way.

In addition to encouraging the pastoral reader to think of the counseling they do in this way, I have attempted in most of the book to tell them how to do it. I don't believe that what I have said here is the only way, but my attempt has been to be specific enough that pastors can directly use my suggestions to work out their own specific method for counseling. One of the generally understood principles of group leadership is that the less training and experience you have, the more structure you need for conducting the group. Pastoral counseling is really a small group to which that principle should be applied.

Another thing that I have said repeatedly needs to be said once more. A pastoral counselor is not a problem solver. Rather, he provides a relationship in which persons can work on a problem together. The relationship is intended to support and encourage the counselee in her own ability to deal with the problem, just as I have attempted to support and encourage the pastor in doing pastoral counseling. I also encourage the pastor who does much pastoral counseling, even on the short-term basis that we have discussed here, to find a trusted consultant in another helping profession or a professional pastoral counselor and supervisor.

Unlike many books on counseling this one has not emphasized learning from particular cases. It has tried to offer a way of proceeding that can apply to many different kind of cases. It has touched on particular kinds of cases in the last two chapters, and even there they have been approached in a more general way. The case approach can be used more effectively if a pastor goes on for further training and supervision in counseling.

Finally, although I have used very little theological language in this book, I think it has probably been clear that my emphasis on the pastor's relational wisdom is based upon a theological conviction that Christian pastoral care and counseling is based on a belief in a God who has chosen to be in relationship with humankind and who holds us in God's memory. Pastors offer care and counseling with the conviction that what they do is an expression of the care of a remembering God.

Resources for Further Reading

Churchill, Larry R. "Narrative Awareness in Ethics Consultations: The Consultant as Story-Maker." In "Narrative Ethics: The Role of Stories in Bioethics," edited by Montello, Martha. Special issue, *Hastings Center Report* 44 (January–February 2014): S36–S39.

Doherty, William J. *Putting Family First: Successful Strategies for Reclaiming Family Life in a Hurry-Up World.* New York: Henry Holt and Company, 2002.

————. *Take Back Your Marriage: Sticking Together in a World That Pulls Us Apart.* New York: The Guilford Press, 2001.

Gottman, John M. *The Relationship Cure: The 5 Step Guide to Strengthening Your Marriage, Family, and Friendships.* New York: Harmony Books, 2001.

Messer, Neil. *Flourishing: Health, Disease, and Bioethics in Theological Perspective.* Grand Rapids, MI: Wm. B. Eerdmans, 2013.

Montello, Martha, ed. "Narrative Ethics: The Role of Stories in Bioethics." Special issue, *Hastings Center Report* 44 (January–February 2014).

Orr, Robert D. *Medical Ethics and the Faith Factor: A Handbook for Clergy and Heath-Care Professionals.* Grand Rapids, MI: William B. Eerdmans, 2009.

Patton, John. *Pastoral Care: An Essential Guide.* Nashville: Abingdon Press, 2003.

Bibliography

Berger, Peter. *Facing Up to Modernity: Excursions in Society, Politics, and Religion*. New York: Basic Books, 1977.

Brueggemann, Walter. *Theology of the Old Testament: Testimony, Dispute, Advocacy*. Minneapolis, MN: Augsburg/Fortress, 1997.

Churchill, Larry R. "Narrative Awareness in Ethics Consultations: The Consultant as Story-Maker." In "Narrative Ethics: The Role of Stories in Bioethics," edited by Martha Montello. Special issue, *Hastings Center Report* 44 (January–February 2014): S36–S39.

DeLozier O. L. "Consultation." In *Dictionary of Pastoral Care and Counseling*, Rodney J. Hunter, 223–4. Nashville: Abingdon Press, 1990.

Frank, Arthur. "Narrative Ethics as Dialogical Story-Telling." In "Narrative Ethics: The Role of Stories in Bioethicsm," edited by Martha Montello. Special issue, *Hastings Center Report* 44 (January–February 2014): S16-S20.

Gottman, John M. *The Relationship Cure: A 5 Step Guide to Strengthening Your Marriage, Family, and Friendships*. New York: Harmony Books, 2001.

Gustafson, James M. "Professions as Callings." *Social Service Review* (December 1982): 514.

Malone, Thomas Patrick, and Patrick Thomas Malone. *The Art of Intimacy*. New York: Prentice Hall Press, 1987.

Meilaender, Gilbert. *Bioethics: A Primer for Christians*. 3rd ed. Grand Rapids, MI: Eerdmans, 2013.

Messer, Neil. *Flourishing: Health, Disease, and Bioethics in Theological Perspective*. Grand Rapids, MI: Eerdmans, 2013.

Mitchell, Stephen A. *Relationality: From Attachment to Intersubjectivity*. Relational Perspectives Book Series, vol. 20. New York: Routledge Mental Health, 2010.

Oates, Wayne E. *The Christian Pastor*. Philadelphia: The Westminster Press, 1964.

Orr, Robert D. *Medical Ethics and the Faith Factor: A Handbook for Clergy and Health Care Professionals*. Grand Rapids, MI: Eerdmans, 2009.

Patton, John. *Pastoral Care: An Essential Guide*. Nashville: Abingdon Press, 2005.

———. "Characteristics of the Carers." Chap. 3 in *Pastoral Care in Context: An Introduction to Pastoral Care*. Louisville: Westminster/John Knox, 1993.

Patton, John, and Brian H. Childs. *Caring for Our Generations*. Eugene, OR: Wipf & Stock Publishers, 2007.

Schachtel, Earnest G. "On Memory and Childhood Amnesia." *A Study of Interpersonal Relations*, edited by Patrick Mullahy, 12. New York: Hermitage Press, 1949.

Schenck, David, and Larry Churchill. *Healers: Extraordinary Clinicians at Work*. New York: Oxford University Press, 2012.

Smith, David H., ed. *Caring Well: Religion, Narrative, and Health Care Ethics*. Louisville: Westminster John Knox Press, 2000.

Wood, Charles M. "Vision and Discernment." Chap. 4 in *Vision and Discernment: An Orientation in Theological Study*. Atlanta: Scholars Press, 1985.

Wynne, Lyman, and Adele Wynne. "The Quest for Intimacy." *Journal of Marital and Family Therapy* 12, no. 4 (1986): 383-94.

Printed in the USA
CPSIA information can be obtained
at www.ICGtesting.com
LVHW030139230824
789062LV00013B/505

9 781630 886905